Neil Harris

THE BEST PUBS IN LAKELAND

ALSO BY MIKE DUNN

The Penguin Guide to Real Draught Beer

Birmingham Pubs 1880–1939
(with Alan Crawford and Robert Thorne)

Local Brew

Walking Through the Lake District

Walking Ancient Trackways

The Lake District

This guide would have been much the poorer without the comments, recommendations and dedicated sampling of CAMRA members in Cumbria, in particular Graham Donning, George Nicholson, Brian Quayle, Alison Cross, Alan Welsh and Stuart Lowe. I'd also like to thank those landlords who put up with my questioning, or in some cases put me up for the night, whilst I carried out my own research. I hope you enjoy their pubs as much as I did. Finally, a word for the equally dedicated team back at home – my wife Chris and daughters Katie and Sarah – who put a lot of effort into persuading me to finish the book so that I could get on with something more useful!

Mike Dunn

THE BEST PUBS IN Lakeland

Mike Dunn

Illustrated by Phil Evans

ALMA BOOKS

IN ASSOCIATION WITH THE CAMPAIGN FOR REAL ALE

Author : **Mike Dunn**

Design : **Opus**

Illustrations : **Phil Evans**

Cover photograph of The Wasdale Head Inn : **Neil Hanson**

Typeset and printed by : **Cambridge University Press**

ISBN **1–85249–016–0**

Published by **Alma Books Ltd.,** *a wholly-owned subsidiary of the Campaign for Real Ale Ltd., 34 Alma Road, St Albans, Herts.*

CONTENTS

INTRODUCTION

THE BEST VIEW

One of the best of all the pub games played in the Lake District – and perhaps the only one peculiar to the region – requires no special apparatus and doesn't take up too much room. All that's needed is for someone to enquire innocently of the assembled company what the best view in Lakeland might be. Opinions differ, the temperature rises and (at least on one memorable occasion when the Workington Brewery's late, lamented John Peel ales were flowing steadily) fists fly. In another book I've listed some of the regular contenders for the title of best view, including Windermere from Orrest Head, the panorama southwards from Skiddaw Little Man, and the mountains encircling the hamlet of Wasdale Head. My own contender, for what it's worth, is the view down Newlands from the magnificent slate summit cairn on Dale Head.

No-one can 'win' such a contest, of course, but one interesting fact to emerge is that a surprisingly high proportion of these views are enhanced by one of the most delightful of man's contributions to the landscape, the pub. The last two listed above, for example: from many vantage points on the fellsides above Wasdale the centrepiece of the hamlet of Wasdale Head, the old Wastwater Hotel (now renamed the Wasdale Head Inn) features prominently in the view, while a distant whitewashed building in the Dale Head panorarna is the excellent Swinside Inn, beckoning the fellwalker but a thirsty two-hour tramp away. There are many more, notably the Old Dungeon Ghyll Hotel in its peerless position beneath the unmistakable skyline of the Langdale Pikes. Not all, however, are dalehead hotels; others make a more subtle contribution to the landscape, as with the Britannia next to Elterwater's pocket-handkerchief village green, or the half-timbered Blue Bell at Heversham. There are classic town pubs, too, such as the extravagantly tiled Howard Arms in Carlisle and the solid stone Hole in't Wall in Bowness.

THE BEST PUBS

In this book we present the finest pubs in the Lake District – in our opinion, of course, for there is plenty of room for debate over which to include and which to leave out. Every one of the 123 selected, however unassuming, is someone's favourite, and every apparently flawless pub has its faults, however tiny, and its detractors, however apparently misguided. So this is not a guide only to bars in dalehead hotels, or oak-beamed country inns, or, for that matter, street-corner locals. It covers all of these and many other sub-classes of that most varied of species, the English pub, but seeks out the best of them, and only the best.

It hasn't been easy, of course, even though the fieldwork (!) has been a treat. In towns like Keswick, or even in the larger villages, difficult choices have had to be made. Some landlords will be disappointed that their pub has not been included (others, ironically, might prefer that theirs had been left out). But this is an honest, unbiased attempt to find the pubs which visitors will want to go to, will enjoy themselves in, and above all will remember. They all, naturally, sell a decent pint of traditional draught beer – real ale – but they have very little else in common; perhaps the only feature they share is the ability to provide a friendly welcome, that invaluable knack of putting the visitor at ease.

What, then, is the drinking tourist at large in the Lake District likely to find in the collection of pubs in this book, apart from handpumps on the bar and a large smile on the landlord's face? And perhaps just as important, what should he (or she) seek to avoid? To answer the first question first, he will find a tremendous variety of places to call in at, whether for a drink, for a meal, or for a bed for the night. Those seeking drink will be able to choose from the unpretentious, such as the Farmers Arms in Portinscale, the boisterous, as in the Old Dungeon Ghyll's public bar, those purveying old-fashioned comfort, including the Bower House in Eskdale, and the almost opulent, such as the Crown at Wetheral. The average quality of food served has improved considerably over the last few years, and there are some particularly interesting pub restaurants, including the Old Crown in Hesket Newmarket and Mason's Arms on Cartmel Fell. And the variety of accommodation is notable too – though it often proves to be the case that simple, homely pubs are at least as good, in value-for-money terms, as the more expensive hotels. There's a similar variety of gardens, too, varying from a few tables dotted around outside the pub to whole fields, some with children's play equipment and many with a marvellous view – for example, the Coledale Inn at Braithwaite near Keswick, with a wonderful panorama including Skiddaw across Bassenthwaite Lake.

THE WORST PUBS

What the drinking tourist will also find is a surprising number of 'unimproved' pubs – not the classic unspoilt gems which we all trust will remain so, but cold, unwelcoming spartan boozers with rickety seating, awful beer, and a two-day old cheese cob on offer. Yes, they do exist – oddly enough, more in the southern Lakes than the north – but not in this book. He might find pubs tied to a particular brewery and therefore cajoled into selling one beer rather than another – even into selling a keg beer through handpumps in the hope of boosting trade. He might delight at finding a 'free' house only to discover that a brewer has lent money to the landlord and now dictates what he sells, restricting his choice and therefore his customers' freedom quite unreasonably. He might find a pub ripped apart and completely remodelled internally in the name of progress – but progress which nobody who actually uses the pub appears to want. There are some great pubs in Cumbria, but some bad ones too.

Even bad pubs are (just) better than no pubs at all, though. In the Lake District as elsewhere there has been a gradual decline in the number of pubs and some classic locals have been lost. This is bad enough in towns such as Kendal (where the impending loss of the Golden Lion in the Market Place is an absolute tragedy) but disastrous in villages threatened with the loss of their only pub. Local breweries have certainly had a pretty good record on this issue, and Jennings of Cockermouth were rightly regarded in the early 1980s as more adept than most at keeping open the tiniest and most remote of country pubs. Breweries have been known to change their policies, however, and Jennings have certainly sold some of their smaller rural pubs since then – the wonderfully unspoilt Blue Bell at Embleton, for example, has been a private house since 1986 – whilst keeping others, such as the timeless Black Cock at Eaglesfield, very much alive. Of course sometimes there is no alternative; but just occasionally one wonders whether the accountant has out-talked those in the brewery with a social conscience.

BREWERIES

Not only pubs but also breweries have been lost in recent years, with the Old Brewery in Carlisle and the Workington Brewery closed, with the loss of locally-brewed ales, in fairly bizarre circumstances following multiple changes of ownership – and in Workington's case following a period as the Lakeland Lager Brewery! Now there are only two long-established breweries in the county, Hartley's of Ulverston (themselves taken over in 1982 but still producing plenty of real ale) and Jennings of Cockermouth. In addition there are two newer ventures – Yates of Westnewton near Aspatria, whose bitter is as least as good as any you'll find in the Lake District, and the Old Crown in Hesket Newmarket, which has recently joined the ranks of pubs brewing their own beers, with two highly individual ales on offer.

There are, however, a number of notable brews from outside the county available in the Lake District's pubs. Particular mention should be made of Mitchells of Lancaster, whose excellent beers just brush the southern fringes of the area, Thwaites, Marston's and Vaux. And there are also the real ales, generally a good deal blander, of the national brewers, particularly Scottish & Newcastle, whose beers include not only the unexciting McEwan's and Younger's but also (as a result of a recent takeover) Matthew Brown and Theakston's, the latter notorious for its dark, strong Old Peculier. S & N received their comeuppance in October 1988, when they themselves were on the receiving end of a takeover bid, from Elders IXL, who already own Courage. The outcome was still awaited when this guide went to press; sadly one can conceive of no outcome which will actually improve the lot of the beer drinker. Finally, honourable mention should be made of free houses such as the Mason's Arms on Cartmel Fell, the Drunken Duck near Ambleside and the Crown at Broadfield, south of Carlisle, which offer a notably wide variety of 'guest' beers to the great delight of their customers.

REAL ALE

Much has been made in preceding paragraphs of the virtues of real ale; but what exactly is it? Essentially it is beer which has been brewed, stored and served in the traditional manner. At the brewery it is brewed from natural ingredients – malted barley, hops, yeast and water. Once fermented it is racked into casks, primed with a little sugar in order to encourage a secondary fermentation, and left to mature; this conditioning, so essential to development of subtle flavours, is cut short in keg beers by chilling, filtering and pasteurisation. In the pub the beer is either served direct from the cask 'by gravity' (rare in the Lake District but occasionally seen with strong ales such as Old Tom in Hartley's pubs) or drawn from the cask by beer engine – the common-or-garden handpump – or by electric pump (again rare in the Lake District).

Keg beers and British lagers, on the other hand, already with much of the goodness taken out by chilling and filtering (and in any case quite often brewed from inferior materials), are further chilled in the pub and then pushed from the keg by carbon dioxide pressure. The low temperature and high gas content serve to mask the lack of flavour. The result is pure liquid mediocrity – a clear, fizzy and virtually tasteless concoction.

MILD AND BITTER

Real British beer, however, though it may occasionally disappoint (usually because either the brewer or publican has cut corners), still has a wide variety of styles and at its best is a superb, palate-tingling experience. The basic draught styles are bitter, usually light-coloured, and mild, usually much darker (though there are darkish bitters, including Jennings, which are actually a good deal darker than many light milds!). Mild ale has been in decline for many years now, hampered by its cloth-cap image and also, perhaps, by its less distinctive taste (less well-hopped and therefore characteristically somewhat blander than bitter, and also a little weaker on average). Nevertheless there are some excellent milds remaining, and Jennings' own mild is not a bad example, though it is in by no means all of their pubs. Marston's Merrie Monk, occasionally available in one or two of the pubs in this book, is amongst the strongest in the country and has a unique taste.

Bitter, though, is the great British beer, although there is enormous variation from one part of the country to another and even between different breweries in the same town. The sweeter beers of the Midlands, for example, contrast sharply with the subtle, bitter beers of the south-east and the smooth, creamy north-eastern bitters. Equally there are differences in colour, from light straw-coloured bitters to golden, reddish and even maroon hues. And there is a gradation from low gravity 'boy's bitter', weak but sometimes refreshing and ideal quaffing ales, through standard, medium-strength beers to the top-of-the-range premium bitters and strong ales. In the Lake District ordinary bitters are provided by Jennings and Hartley's (who produce two including the newly-introduced Fellrunners); and Hartley's also brew the renowned and very satisfying XB premium bitter. Stronger beers include Vaux Samson and Marston's Pedigree, though the strongest widely available in the Lakes is the famous and unusual Theakston's Old Peculier, with its peculiar spelling and very peculiar effects on some: it is certainly to be handled with care!

Mike Dunn

HOW TO USE THIS GUIDE

The guide is divided into nine areas (see contents list). The pubs are listed alphabetically according to the town or village in which they are situated (or if isolated, the nearest centre of population). The practical details for each pub are given in the left column and symbols are used to give the following information:

food is available as specified. This always means full meals; other pubs without the symbol may well serve snacks. Many pubs do not serve meals late in the evening, so check by phone if you wish to eat late.

a garden, or where specified, other outdoor area for drinking – occasionally this will just be tables on the pavement.

a family room or area without a bar is provided where the licensee will allow children accompanied by a parent or other responsible adult. In pubs where meals are served, children may be confined to the dining area, and thus be expected to have a meal. Check with staff.

the type of accommodation is specified in the text, and ranges from three-star hotels which sell real ale, to more modest pubs with bedrooms or self-catering facilities. No prices are given. Check by phone for availability.

real ales are listed with beers from independent breweries given first, then national brands. For full details of local beers see the brewery section on p 15 or consult CAMRA's Good Beer Guide.

PUB HOURS

In August 1988 the British Government made long-overdue changes to pub licensing laws, which had been severely restricted since the First World War. Pubs can now open Monday to Saturday from 11 am until 11 pm. But individual licensees can choose which hours they wish to open between 11 in the morning and 11 at night. They will choose their hours to suit their trade. Many pubs now display their opening hours on the exterior. The changes came too late to monitor their effect for this guide but it is likely that pubs in tourist areas or areas of high urban concentration will stay open in the afternoon, especially in the summer. During the winter months it is likely that many pubs will keep to the old hours and will close between 3 pm and 5.30 or 6 pm. Sunday hours have been only slightly extended: the standard hours are 12 noon to 3 pm and 7 pm to 10.30 pm.

CHILDREN IN PUBS

You cannot drink alcohol in a pub below the age of eighteen years (although at sixteen, children with adults may drink beer, cider or wine with a meal). You can go into a pub at fourteen but you can drink only non-alcoholic products. Licensees tend to be extremely strict on "under-age drinking" as they can be prosecuted and lose their licences to trade. Children of all ages can go into pubs that have rooms set aside as "family rooms". They can also eat in pubs that have rooms used as restaurants. If a pub in this guide is shown to have a beer garden then children can use this facility but if the garden is reached via the pub it is wise for parents or guardians to ask permission to take the children through the licensed area.

THE BREWERS

There's still a good choice of beer in the Lake District, despite the depredations of the national brewers. Two local breweries have stood the test of time (though one is now the subsidiary of a Manchester brewer) and two new, necessarily small-scale, ventures have joined them. The bitter brewed by one of the newcomers, Yates of Westnewton, is an outstanding addition to the scene, worth tracking down in free house outlets such as the George in Keswick and the Wasdale Head Inn. And beers from several other notable brewers can be found in particular outlets.

However, too many of the pubs in Cumbria are now controlled by Scottish and Newcastle – not just those selling the mediocre McEwan and Younger ales, but also, as a result of a recent takeover, Matthew Brown and Theakston pubs. The takeover bid by Elders IXL for S and N, announced in October 1988 and unresolved when this guide went to press, will hardly help to widen choice either. Beer drinkers will fervently hope that Theakston's beers, in particular, not only survive – who would want to drink Younger's IPA if this were to be foisted onto pubs as a replacement for Theakston's delicious XB? – but are also allowed to retain their present character and distinctiveness instead of being turned into bland and boring beers designed to suit, or at least not to offend, a 'national' palate. A full list of the real ales which can be tried in the best pubs in the Lake District is given below, with a description of the brewer, the beer name, its original gravity, and a comment (inevitably subjective) on the style and quality of the beer. The original gravity figure – for example 1040 – is a good guide to strength and, when compared with relative prices, of the value-for-money of different beers. Essentially it is a measure of the amount of raw materials used in brewing the beer, as a proportion of the amount of water used. Thus a 1040 beer comprises 40 parts of fermentable material to 1000 parts of water. The weakest beers brewed tend to have a gravity of 1030 or so; 1037 is an average strength for ordinary bitter; 1040 to 1045 covers most strong bitters; and 1070 to 1080 strong ales and barley wines.

BASS of Burton-on-Trent and Tadcaster

The beers come from Bass North, the trading company of the massive Bass organisation in northern England. SPECIAL BITTER (1036) Sadly, nothing to write home about. DRAUGHT BASS (1044) A pale shadow of a once-great brew.

BROUGHTON BREWERY of Biggar, Lanarkshire

Set up in 1980 by a former Scottish and Newcastle executive, this has become one of the most significant of the new breweries, not least because it shows S and N and others the way to irrigate the Scottish beer desert. GREENMANTLE ALE (1038) A very palatable, quite sweet and darkish bitter beer.

MATTHEW BROWN of Blackburn

A brewery which heroically defended its independence against Scottish and Newcastle in 1985 only to fall to a renewed bid in 1987. Brown did, however, blot their own copybook by taking over Theakston in 1984 and then closing the latter's Carlisle brewery. Now Brown's Workington brewery has also been axed, and John Peel bitter, the best beer brewed in Blackburn, has also been withdrawn. MILD (1031) Somewhat thin-tasting, but at its best a delicate nutty-flavoured dark brew. BITTER (1036) A malty and quite pleasant beer.

HARTLEY of Ulverston

Taken over by Robinson in 1982, but still brewing and still supplying real ale to all fifty-six tied pubs in and around the southern Lake District. A new beer, Fellrunners, was introduced in October 1988, reputedly to fill the gap between ordinary bitter and XB, though the future of ordinary bitter must now be doubtful. MILD (1031) A quite pleasant smooth dark mild. BITTER (1031) An extremely light-tasting beer which has its devotees in and around Ulverston; not by any means in all the pubs. FELLRUNNERS (1035) A very well-hopped and quite dark bitter brew which deserves to succeed despite its name. XB (1040) Malty, full-bodied and distinctive, an excellent premium bitter which is very popular in the free trade.

HESKET NEWMARKET BREWERY

A new venture into brewing by the owners of the Old Crown in the village. At present the beers are WRYNOSE LIGHT BITTER and BLENCATHRA BITTER, both of them highly distinctive and certainly worth a try; but at this early stage in the brewery's development there may well be changes in store for the beers.

IND COOPE of Burton-on-Trent

A subsidiary of the giant Allied Breweries. BURTON ALE (1047) One of Allied's very few noteworthy real ales, Burton Ale is strong and distinctive, with a refreshingly hoppy taste.

JENNINGS of Cockermouth

The second of the Lake District's remaining long-established brewers. The brewery nestles in a picturesque setting beneath Cockermouth Castle. Real ale is available in all seventy-six tied houses plus a fair free trade. Beware hand-pumped Lakeland Light – despite appearances this is a (very weak) keg beer. MILD (1034) A malty and quite full-flavoured beer, medium-dark and smooth-tasting. BITTER (1034) A really distinctive beer which is much darker than most bitters, with a malty tang but quite a bitter aftertaste.

McEWAN of Edinburgh

Part of Scottish and Newcastle (currently the target of a bid from Elders IXL), as is Younger. 70/- (also sold as YOUNGER SCOTCH or XXPS) (1036) A dull, middle-of-the-road bitter. 80/- (also sold as YOUNGER IPA) (1042) Heavier but still bland. YOUNGER NO. 3 (1043) A dark ale with a proud history.

MARSTON of Burton-on-Trent

A major regional brewery with pubs from Cumbria to Hampshire following a series of takeovers. Brews a very wide range of real ales (not all of them available in the Lake District). BURTON BITTER (1037) A fine ordinary bitter, a splendidly refreshing brew which is highly regarded. PEDIGREE (1043) Advertised as 'the king of bitters' and rightly so: this is a full-bodied, pale and delicate premium bitter. Subtly-flavoured and quite strong, it is one of the best bitters in the country. MERRIE MONK (1043) a highly unusual strong dark mild, rich and sweet but otherwise not too dissimilar to Pedigree. OWD RODGER (1080) A magnificent draught barley wine, very dark, rather sweet, rich and satisfying.

MITCHELLS of Lancaster

An underrated local brewery company, now brewing in the former Yates and Jackson brewery. It owns fifty pubs, a few of them in south-east Cumbria. MILD (1034) A smooth, creamy brew which was once so popular in Mitchells' rural pubs that it was known as Country Mild. BITTER (1036) Nutty and malty yet refreshingly dry; made from Yorkshire pale-ale malt.

ROBINSON of Stockport

An expanding Greater Manchester brewery which bought Hartley of Ulverston in 1982. Robinson's beers are now available in some of these pubs as well as in the free trade. BEST BITTER (1041) A great bitter, very pale indeed but well-hopped and with a delicate but distinctive flavour. OLD TOM (1080) One of the very few classic draught strong ales still with us, this is a darkish brew which is smooth but not too sweet, at its most popular in winter.

RUDDLES of Oakham

Formerly a proudly independent real ale brewer, now a subsidiary of Grand Metropolitan, the owners of Watney. BEST BITTER (1037) A standard bitter. COUNTY (1050) A once-great beer which has lost character in recent years.

JOHN SMITH of Tadcaster

The northern arm of Courage, now owned by Elders IXL, the company run by Australian tycoon John Elliott. BITTER (1036) A fairly pleasant session beer.

TENNENT of Edinburgh

The Scottish arm of Bass, with virtually no interest in promoting real ale. 80/- (1042) a full-flavoured ale, rarely available in 'real' form.

TETLEY of Leeds

Yet another subsidiary company, this time (like Ind Coope) part of Allied Breweries. MILD (1032) A noticeably malty brew, dark and rather thin-tasting. BITTER (1035) Regarded as one of the better northern bitters, but with rather less flavour than some of its competitors; nevertheless a creamy and well-balanced brew.

THEAKSTON of Masham (North Yorkshire) and Newcastle

A famous Yorkshire brewery which sadly surrendered its independence to Matthew Brown in 1984, only to find itself part of Scottish and Newcastle as a result of a further outbreak of merger mania. BEST BITTER (1037) A pale and still distinctive ordinary bitter. XB (1044) A very good premium bitter, full of flavour, which was introduced in 1982. OLD PECULIER (1057) Named after the eighteenth-century Peculier of Masham, brewed from a mash including malt extract, caramel and maize, but also dry-hopped to add a touch of bitterness. Slightly weakened in recent years, but still a unique strong dark ale.

THWAITES of Blackburn

A strongly traditional Lancashire brewery, renowned for its superb mild ales. Took over Yates and Jackson of Lancaster in 1984 to increase its strength in south Cumbria. BEST MILD (1032) A medium-dark malty brew which is quite rightly held in high regard. BITTER (1036) Well-hopped but not especially distinctive.

VAUX of Sunderland

One of the larger regional brewers, but one which has closed a number of breweries recently. LORIMERS SCOTCH (1036) Pleasant and malty, but less distinctive than when it was brewed at Lorimer and Clark, Vaux's former subsidiary in Edinburgh. BITTER (1038) The eagerly awaited new brew from Vaux, but disappointingly bland. SAMSON (1042) Long-established and an old favourite, this is a robust, quite dark and distinctively sharp, clean-tasting bitter.

WARD of Sheffield

A subsidiary of Vaux, with a clutch of tied houses in South Yorkshire and a much more extensive free trade, plus guest appearances in other Vaux group pubs. SHEFFIELD BEST BITTER (1038) Quite robust and full-flavoured though rather sweet, this is a popular standard bitter.

WEBSTER of Halifax

The northern brewery of the Watney/Grand Metropolitan combine, which since the closure of Wilson's Manchester brewery in 1986 has also tried to 'match' the latter's beers. WILSON'S ORIGINAL MILD (1032) A malty but rather ordinary mild. WILSON'S ORIGINAL BITTER (1036) Well-balanced but without distinction. WEBSTER'S YORKSHIRE BITTER (1036) A bland, utterly unmemorable brew. WEBSTER'S CHOICE (1045) A somewhat fuller-bodied premium bitter.

WHITBREAD of Castle Eden

Castle Eden is one of Whitbread's very few remaining traditional breweries, and its future has been in doubt for years. CASTLE EDEN ALE

(1040) A rather pleasant if slightly sweet full-bodied bitter.

WILSON: see Webster

YATES of Westnewton, near Aspatria

A new brewery set up in 1986 by Peter Yates, formerly head brewer with Jennings, at Ghyll Farm, Westnewton. Ghyll Farm was a 'jerry' or home-brew pub at the turn of the century; now the brewing plant has been installed in a barn which was once the home of the farm's goats. BITTER (1035) A superb, light-coloured and dry bitter beer which is deceptively full-bodied.

YOUNGER: see McEwan

Elderly local noting similarity of clientele

The area around Kendal and Windermere, often billed as the gateway to the Lake District, is an area of tremendous contrasts, with the most popular holiday destinations such as Bowness and Windermere town creaking under the weight of countless tourists, yet within a few miles real solitude can be found in the low rolling hills around Cartmel Fell to the east of Lake Windermere. There is also the historic market town of Kendal and the Morecambe Bay 'coastline' around the highly individual little resort of Grange-over-Sands.

By all means visit Bowness, with its pier serving the lake steamers, its promenade and its theatre (and don't forget the Hole in't Wall, an essential stop for the drinking tourist), but escape to the superb viewpoint at Gummers How for a relatively uncrowded spot from which to savour the panorama over Lake Windermere to the Coniston Fells and the instantly recognisable Langdale Pikes. Windermere is, in fact, a lake of three distinct sections, with its crowded northern and surprisingly quiet southern basins separated by a shallow middle reach around the interesting, wooded Belle Isle. From here, or from Fell Foot country park (a recent addition to the list of attractions hereabouts, with bathing, boat hire and an adventure playground) at the southern end of the lake it is a short journey to Cartmel, notable for its village square and massive priory church, and then on to the Kent estuary and Grange-over-Sands, with its promenade looking out over the muddy sands of Morecambe Bay to the Lancashire coast.

Northwards from Grange lies the fascinating and little-known area of the Winster and Lyth valleys – damsons are a notable delicacy in autumn here – with dramatic landscapes of limestone pavement and wide views in all directions. The little rocky hills and dells around Cartmel Fell's secluded church are quite delightful – and this area also has the benefit of the Mason's Arms, one of the truly outstanding pubs in the Lake District. Then Kendal, a medieval wool town with attractive cobbled streets and enclosed yards, a ruined castle on a green hill overlooking the town, a splendid museum and art gallery, and a selection of delightful pubs.

All this plus walking too – for the Kentmere valley and Longsleddale, with excellent walks starting from the dalehead hamlets, are within easy reach. Sadgill in Longsleddale, with the sparkling River Sprint running beneath a classic packhorse bridge, is the start of little-known but exhilarating walks in the far eastern fells. Kentmere village is a particularly rewarding spot, with a striking medieval pele tower now incorporated in a farmhouse, and the Garburn Road, a famous old packhorse track, starting its rocky journey to Troutbeck here. The Garburn Road is also the first stage of a challenging fellwalking expedition, the Kentmere Round, which circles the dalehead and includes the summits of Yoke, Ill Bell, Froswick, Harter Fell and Kentmere Pike.

BOWNESS-ON-WINDERMERE
Hole in't Wall [New Hall]

Tel: Windermere (096 62) 3488
Robinson Place

✕ lunchtime and evening

Hartley Mild, Fellrunners, XB

The first pub in this book is also one of the very best. It's a magnificent crowded bar tucked away in Robinson Place, a quiet back street near the lake. The Hole in't Wall, correctly but very rarely referred to as the New Hall Inn, is reputedly the oldest inn in Bowness, and it is claimed that Charles Dickens drank here (which, as Lake District regulars will know, at least makes a pleasant change from the usual claims to a Wordsworth connection). Another notable here was Thomas Longmire, the landlord of the Hole in't Wall and also the champion wrestler of England in the 1850s. It's certainly easy to see what attracted them. There is a huge open fireplace with logs stacked high on either side; an impressive, irregular bar counter; and comfortable seating around the walls. One part of the ceiling is ornately carved, while another is host to a dozen or so chamberpots. Behind the bar is a collection of banknotes, while a side room caters for those addicted to pool and rock music. The food has a heavy accent on the home made (including quiches) and there is also a wide variety of omelettes. Outside the pub is a small patio, useful for those with children in tow; but the real fun lies inside this lively, mildly eccentric pub. Don't miss it!

BURTON-IN-KENDAL
King's Arms

Tel: Burton (0524) 781409
Main Street (A6070).

✕ lunchtime and evening

Mitchells Mild, Best Bitter

A thriving village pub with a dedicated local following, the King's Arms is built in the classic northern tradition, with a long entrance hall leading directly towards the bar counter and rooms leading off on both sides. Modernisation has seen some opening out of the original plan, with archways knocked through between some of the individual rooms, but several distinctive drinking areas, each of them serving a well-defined purpose, have been retained. The car park to the rear, with its treacherously uneven cobblestones is, however, definitely unmodernised! A light, spacious room has pub games and a juke box; to the right of the entrace hall is a dining area also patronised by families; and tucked away behind this is a quieter area, with a welcoming real fire, close to the bar counter. Much of the serious drinking tends to be done standing up in the central lobby and its various alcoves. Food is available at virtually all times, and the menu includes tasty if not especially authentic curries. The accommodation is simple but inexpensive, and the full breakfast is likely to satisfy even the biggest appetite. Burton today is a large, mainly residential village close to the motorway and main line railway (the Beeching-axed Holme & Burton station is a mile north of the village). It's hard to believe that during the eighteenth century the corn market here was the most extensive in England.

CARTMEL
King's Arms

Tel: Cartmel (044 854) 220
Market Place

- lunchtime and evening
- **Marston Pedigree; Whitbread Castle Eden Ale**

Cartmel's market place, with the priory gatehouse and former prior's refectory (now an hotel), is the centrepiece of a really delightful place, adjudged best-kept village in Cumbria on several occasions. The King's Arms, a well-proportioned eighteenth-century building, makes its own contribution to the local environment, with climbing roses around the ground floor windows, and flowers in tubs on just about every conceivable surface, including the old mounting steps to one side of the front door and even the roof of the porch. All this forms a backdrop to a cobbled patio, with several rustic tables and benches. And to the side of the pub can be seen wooden barrels dating from the era (only recently ended in this part of the world) when the local real ale came from the wood. Today, Marston's Pedigree (a new addition in the last few months) is available in the cosy bar and equally cosy beamed lounge with its impressive grandfather clock. At the end of the passage is a quite big, respectable children's room. Morning coffee and a selection of hot and cold food are available. Despite the steady flow of tourists through Cartmel in search of the impressive priory church the King's Arms has managed to stay as it should: a really unspoilt, traditional village inn. Long may it remain so.

Pig and Whistle

Tel: Cartmel (044 854) 482
Town End

Hartley XB

This unassuming grey stone pub, the most prominent part of a terrace of houses some distance away from the centre of Cartmel, is extremely popular with local farmers and one can quickly see why: there's a very friendly atmosphere in the long bar with its benches and high-backed chairs, and a pool table for the more energetically inclined. Outside the pub there is an amusing pub sign, with a grotesque orange pig playing the flute, and the frontage is further brightened by a selection of flowers in window boxes. On Bank Holidays it's very likely that a good many of those crowding into the bars will have been to Cartmel Races, an unlikely but highly picturesque venue for National Hunt steeplechasing. Others will probably have strolled down for a pint of Hartley's after a tour of the Priory, an Augustinian foundation dating from 1188. The priory survived the attacks of Robert Bruce, though it was 'desolated' by his army in 1322 (and in the same raids the abbot of Furness was forced to pay a ransom to guarantee his immunity). The main survivals now are the gatehouse and the priory church, with its two towers set diagonally to each other and with surviving medieval glass including John the Baptist and the Virgin and Child. Cartmel Show, a colourful and bustling event held on the second Wednesday in August, is another big event in this historic village.

CARTMEL FELL
Mason's Arms

Tel: Crosthwaite (044 88) 486
Strawberry Bank. OS413895

✕ lunchtime and evening

self-catering flats in adjacent barn

An ever-changing selection of real ales (four available at any one time)

Difficult to find (but no longer *that* difficult – it's now very well known) the Mason's Arms lies at a steep, sharp bend on the road between the beauty spot of Gummers How and Bowland Bridge (and eventually Crosthwaite and Kendal). This excellent old pub takes its name from its former role as the clandestine meeting place of the Kendal Masons towards the end of the eighteenth century. Nowadays it offers a very good choice of traditional draught British beers, an overwhelming range of some 130 bottled beers from Belgium and other foreign parts, and very good meals and snacks, with a menu which is changed daily and includes vegetarian dishes. Outside there's a patio commanding superb views over steeply falling ground to the Winster valley, one of the delightful and relatively little visited valleys between Kendal and Lake Windermere. (Another, the Lyth valley, is better known because of its autumn crop of damsons.) Inside, there are the old world essentials of tiny little rooms with uneven slate floors and low beams – but these are the genuine article, resulting in a pub with a marvellous atmosphere and real character. A big old black-leaded fireplace dominates one room, with its austere wooden tables and ladder-backed chairs, while a varied selection of prints adorns the walls. There's also an oak-panelled lounge. And for those wanting an extended visit there are four self-catering flats in a converted barn just around the corner.

FLOOKBURGH
Crown

Tel: Flookburgh (044 853) 248
Market Street (B5278).

- lunchtime and evening
-
-
- **Hartley Mild, Fellrunners, XB**

Flookburgh is a small fishing village which is situated between the Kent and Leven estuaries, and therefore has wide views over the waters and muddy sands of Morecambe Bay. A highway crosses the sands from nearby Kents Bank to the Lancashire coast, but the services of a guide with knowledge of the local tides, river channels and quicksands are absolutely essential for travellers. Holker Hall, a beautiful country house with formal gardens and a deer park, is just along the road, while Cartmel, with its priory and racecourse, is only a couple of miles away. The Crown is a typical Hartley's pub, a seventeenth-century coaching inn but nowadays essentially an unpretentious village local. It is, however, a pub with a notable history, King Charles II having dined here on a feast of cockles when Flookburgh's third market charter was granted in 1675. Eleven years later much of the town was destroyed by fire, though fortunately the Crown escaped. The public bar has a fine, solid serving counter complete with a set of four venerable handpumps, though only two are in use; it's comfortably furnished in an unelaborate way, and there is also a real fire piled with logs and a collection of toasting forks nearby. Other collections include the inevitable horse brasses and some interesting old beer bottles. There's a separate pool room and family room. The food is really good, with an emphasis on home cooking and vegetarian dishes.

Popular "45° leaning position"

HALE
King's Arms

Tel: Milnthorpe (044 82) 3203
On A6.

✕ lunchtime and evening

Mitchells Best Bitter

For those speeding along the A6 between Kendal and Lancaster the King's Arms is a very useful roadside halt a couple of miles south of Milnthorpe. This is a pretty fast stretch of the road but the pub is easily recognisable because of its coat-of-arms road sign. Beer lovers have the flavoursome bitter from Mitchells of Lancaster – self-styled brewers of 'the best beer' – to enjoy, while there is straightforward but perfectly appetising food on offer seven days a week. The big L-shaped lounge bar, which occupies most of the ground floor, has subdued lighting, lots of dark stained wood, an old-fashioned clock, and a plethora of photographs and prints. Every possible surface, including the inevitable thick oak beams, seems to be pressed into service to display a collection of plates. Above all, there's an unhurried, easygoing atmosphere which makes it a pleasure to call in for a drink here. An archway leads from the lounge into a cosy back snug, with dartboard but few frills, while upstairs there is a lounge set aside for the use of families at lunchtime and until eight o'clock in the evening. Given decent weather the garden is also useful in this respect. It's a caring pub, too: one of the pub's regulars recently spent two weeks walking the Pennine Way to raise money for Cancer Care.

HEVERSHAM
Blue Bell

Tel: Milnthorpe (044 82) 2018
Princes Way (on A6: ignore signs to Heversham village)

✕ lunchtime and evening

Hartley XB; Draught Bass; Tetley Bitter

There must be a few Heversham clerics of old who are whirling in their graves at the changes which have taken place at this former vicarage. Not that the whole project, which has converted a pleasant country inn into a three-star hotel whilst retaining much of the character of the original, hasn't been carried out tastefully and well. But the sixteenth-century black-and-white frontage (which might perhaps be more at home in Herefordshire than here on the fringes of the Lake District) now forms only one part of a considerable enterprise, with the stylish and well-appointed hotel accommodation the centrepiece. The black-and-white theme recurs inside, though in the Cocktail Bar – actually no more than a well-appointed lounge bar – there is a good deal of exposed stonework and dark wood too. It's a highly attractive bar, with subdued lighting, a number of tables intimately located in the window alcoves, and a variety of old photographs on the walls. Here, too, is an imaginative array of bar food which attracts diners from miles around. In contrast, the public bar (the owners are to be applauded on retaining this feature) is relatively spartan, and the family room is surprisingly unexciting too.

HOLME
Smithy

Tel: Burton (0524) 781302
Milnthorpe Road

✕ lunchtime and evening

Thwaites Best Mild, Bitter

Bright and welcoming from the outside, the Smithy is a high-class pub which has been very nicely renovated, with lots of exposed stone pillars and solid wooden beams. The name arises because the pub does indeed incorporate the old village smithy – now the back bar, with seating cleverly provided in the former stalls. The main lounge bar is not short of points of interest. There is a deer's head complete with notable antlers on one wall, and a tapestry beneath on the same theme; a fascinating old beer engine fitted with antique handpumps mounted in a glass case set into a low dividing wall (ironically the draught beer is served by electric pumps!); and, appropriately in this case, horse brasses and sundry equestrian tackle. There's also the original anvil still on show. A fairly standard range of pub food is available seven days a week, and there is a separate children's menu. There are a couple of tables near the front door, which has roses climbing around it; but these are close to a quite busy road, and the tables in the sheltered, pleasantly landscaped courtyard to one side are more popular. Formerly a Yates and Jackson house – sadly their magnificent, very bitter beer, once one of the most distinctive and memorable of British beers, is no longer brewed – the Smithy has airy, spacious bedrooms and is worth considering as an overnight stop on the way to or from the central Lake District.

KENDAL

Brewery Arts Centre

Tel: Kendal (0539) 25133
Highgate

✕ lunchtime

Vaux Samson; Ward Sheffield Best Bitter

Not exactly a pub, but unquestionably one of the best venues for a decent pint in Kendal, this is the bar of an ambitious and highly-praised arts centre which itself is housed in an impressive conversion of the Whitwell, Mark brewery dating from 1853. The Vats Bar is so named because much of the seating is arranged inside the old cedarwood vats (the fermenting vessels where the 'wort' or green beer was matured). The bar is approached through the arts centre foyer, then up a set of stairs which leads to a photographic gallery, and finally past a coffee bar and the Brewery Playgroup (sic). It's definitely worth finding, though, for good beer and interesting lunchtime food – the best perhaps the 'brewery baked' selection – in fascinating surroundings, with a variety of Whitwell, Mark memorabilia on view. Included amongst this are barrel ends and old advertising posters, one of them offering a choice of seven draught beers, the most expensive of them the No. 1 Pale Ale at one shilling and eight pence (8p) a gallon. The heyday of the old brewery was probably the 1930s, when their Auld Kendal ale was supplied throughout Westmorland, but they succumbed to a takeover approach from Vaux of Sunderland in 1948 and the last brew was run through in September 1968. Only four years later the conversion was complete and the arts centre opened its doors to the public.

Duke of Cumberland

Tel: Kendal (0539) 24054
Shap Road (A6)

✕ lunchtime

❀

⊕ **Vaux Bitter, Samson**

The Duke of Cumberland is an excellent local just out of the town centre on the Penrith road but very convenient for the railway station. Also very close are the remains of the thirteenth-century Kendal castle, built on a drumlin (a steep mound of glacial boulder clay). The castle formed part of a medieval deer park, and is now the centrepiece of a pleasant open green area; there is a fine, if somewhat distant, view of the fells in the southern Lake District from the highest point. The Duke of Cumberland has plenty of black beams (some of them looking distinctly warped!) and a lot of exposed stonework, but the prints of foxhounds – one of them spectacularly out-of-focus – and the greenery sprouting in odd corners help to lighten the overall tone. The pub has recently been renovated, the former small bars being knocked through to form one large room, but it nevertheless retains three very separate drinking areas – a front bar much frequented by the domino fraternity, a relaxed back room ideal for a quiet drink or a lunchtime meal, and a middle section which, testimony to the pub's night-time popularity, is entirely devoid of seats. All in all this is a fine, bustling pub with a good local reputation.

Ring o' Bells

Tel: Kendal (0539) 20326
Kirkland

✕ lunchtime

⊕ **Vaux Lorimers Scotch**

An amazing little unspoilt pub abutting onto the churchyard of Holy Trinity, Kendal's parish church, at the southern end of the town centre, the Ring o'Bells has undergone recent renovation but this has been notably restrained and thankfully has left the three-room internal layout untouched. There's a classic northern vault (public bar), with bench seating right round the walls and spartan furnishings – the florid water jug in an alcove seems really out of place. To the right of this is an astonishingly tiny snug with room for just two tables. And to the right again is the lounge bar, offering a good deal more comfort and a variety of hot food at lunchtimes. There's an open fire here and a collection of prints on the walls, and it's even possible that the increasingly rare luxury of table service, for so long a feature here, may yet survive. In the rather windswept yard to the side are three tables for hardier souls. The church, literally next door, has chapels to three local families, including the Parrs – Kendal Castle was the birthplace of Catherine Parr, who became the sixth wife of Henry VIII in 1543. And only a hundred yards or so further into town is Abbot Hall, Kendal's art gallery and also the location of the Museum of Lakeland Life and Industry.

Woolpack [Crown Bar]

Tel: Kendal (0539) 23852
Stricklandgate

✕ lunchtime

🛏

🍺 **Vaux Samson**

The Woolpack, right in the centre of Kendal, is a substantial hotel with full conference and function facilities but with quite a number of surviving traditional features, including the delightful and historic Crown Bar. Kendal was one of the main centres of the Lakeland wool trade and fleeces were brought by packhorse to inns such as the Woolpack (the inn's name says it all). The high archway into the Woolpack's courtyard is another indication of the former importance of the woollen industry here: the arch was specially designed to admit the heavy wagons, piled high with their packs of wool, which replaced packhorses towards the end of the eighteenth century. The Crown Bar dates back to 1740, and at that time it functioned as Kendal's wool auction room – though it is difficult to believe that all the sheep farmers and wool buyers could crowd into this tiny space. The bar now has exposed stonework, an unusual balustraded bar counter and (a favourite spot, no doubt much fought over by the regulars) a comfortable and secluded alcove with a little window. There's also a big arch through to an overspill room, really the reception area for the hotel. Lunchtime food centres around the Carvery, with the roast joint of the day usually very popular.

LEVENS
Hare and Hounds

Tel: Sedgwick (053 95) 60408
A quarter of a mile north of A590

- lunchtime and evening
- at lunchtime
- **Vaux Bitter, Samson**

At the southern (Causeway End) edge of the village and just off the new and very fast road to Barrow, the Hare and Hounds is a well-known village inn with a central bar area serving a number of cosy, low-beamed rooms. There is a distinctive feel to each of the rooms, too, ranging from the former cellar of the pub, which now serves as a typical northern vault and houses the inevitable but undoubtedly popular pool table, to the angled lounge bar, with its comfortable seats, low lighting and intimate nooks and crannies. This latter bar in particular is extremely popular with those in search of food, and there are usually quite a number of family parties in evidence during the season. There's an old-fashioned feel to the place, enhanced by the ancient beams and the archways between the various rooms. The approach to the pub is very pleasant, too, with window boxes and hanging baskets adding a splash of colour, and a number of tables dotted around outside. A more formal, very green and well-kept garden lies to one side. It's a good place to stop and unwind on the way to the Lake District, with the horrors of the motorway journey safely behind. And there is a first bit of sightseeing just around the corner, too: Levens Hall, originally a defensive pele tower but later rebuilt as an Elizabethan mansion, is famous for its topiary, laid out in 1692.

LINDALE
Lindale Inn

Tel: Grange over Sands (044 84) 2416
On B5277, a mile from A590

- ✕ lunchtime and evening
- (icon)
- (icon) if dining
- (icon)
- (icon) **McEwan 70/-; Theakston Best Bitter**

The accent is very definitely on food in this large, solid pub in the centre of the village, and only a mile or so from the main road to Barrow. There is a large, pleasant though very long lounge bar which has been extensively and attractively refurbished, with big wooden tables and plush seating. Old beer bottles are on display and there are exposed beams for the traditionalist. The Theakston's beer is very acceptable and although the menus are not especially out of the ordinary there is a good choice including some local specialities. In addition to the food, there is modern accommodation and a large function room: live music is regularly presented. Outside drinking is quite popular – weather permitting, of course – in the shadow of the big, white-painted pub itself. Lindale, admittedly a village of distinctly limited intrinsic interest, is nevertheless a useful centre for touring the south-eastern fringes of the Lake District, including the curious little resort of Grange-over-Sands, the hidden valleys of the Lyth and Winster and Kendal and the Kent valley. The southern end of Windermere is not very far away either.

NEWBY BRIDGE
Newby Bridge Inn

Tel: Newby Bridge (053 95) 31222
On A590

- ✕ lunchtime and evening
- (icon)
- (icon)
- (icon)
- (icon) **Younger Scotch Bitter**

The smaller of the two hotels facing each other across Newby Bridge on the River Leven, the Newby Bridge Inn is nevertheless very well appointed, with restyled accommodation including family rooms and even a four poster room. The hotel is set back away from the main road in its own grounds, with picnic tables on a manicured lawn at the front, overlooking the river. The Leven at this point, as it passes under the attractive arched bridge, is wide and relatively slow-moving and boats are available for hire. The foot of Lake Windermere, with its lake steamers, is a little further away, while the Lakeside and Haverthwaite steam railway runs through Newby Bridge on its way to the lake.

The inn's lounge bar, nicely furnished, is split into three areas, with a pool table at one end and the bar counter at the other, facing perhaps the pleasantest of the drinking areas, with a stone fireplace and tables around the big picture windows. There is a superb range of bar food (a wider range of draught beer would not go amiss!), and an elegant separate dining room. It's a good base from which to explore the hidden treasures and relatively gentle scenery of the southern Lake District.

This area of low fells, woodlands and fascinating little towns and villages is often unjustly neglected by tourists heading for the central fells, or passing through on their way to the western dales, but it amply repays a more leisurely exploration. Grizedale Forest, for example, is far from typical of Forestry Commission forests: in addition to a varied selection of forest trails, including the Silurian Way, there's an excellent visitor centre south of Hawkshead, with exhibition area, children's playground and the renowned Theatre in the Forest. South from here is the secluded village of Satterthwaite and the valley of the Rusland Pool, beautifully unspoilt and with an important nature reserve at Rusland Moss.

From here it is easy to cut across to Cunsey, where there is an early iron smelting site at the end of a simple but attractive walk, and then to take the road along the uncrowded western shores of Lake Windermere, passing Low Stott Park, where one of the last surviving bobbin mills in the Lake District has been carefully converted into a working museum, before arriving at Lakeside – terminus for the Lakeside and Haverthwaite steam railway and also for the lake steamers which travel the length of Windermere, calling at Bowness and Waterhead, near Ambleside. Also worth a visit in this area are the former market centre of Bouth (don't forget to call in at the White Hart here!) and Colton, with its notable church standing in splendid isolation.

Further south is the bustling town of Ulverston, probably at its most attractive when the livestock market is in full swing on Thursdays, although there are also some stalls selling local produce in Market Street on Saturdays. Worth a visit are Hoad Hill, crowned by a lighthouse which acts as a memorial to Sir John Barrow, a local lad who went on to become Under-Secretary to the Admiralty, and the remains of the short canal, now largely silted up, which connected Ulverston to the sea during the town's brief period of huge prosperity as a port in the early nineteenth century, when iron ore, slate and locally manufactured goods were exported. The canal basin, complete with wild-fowl, still exists together with Brow Bridge Lock and the pier at Canal Foot, forlornly looking out over Cartmel Sands and the Leven estuary.

Mention should also be made of Furness Abbey, a major landowner in the southern Lake District during the medieval period and now a tourist attraction in its own right. The abbey was founded by Stephen, later to become King of England, in 1123; originally it belonged to the Order of Savigny but it eventually came under the control of the Cistercians. The extensive remains lie beneath red sandstone cliffs in a sheltered wooded valley on the outskirts of Barrow-in-Furness. And we've thoughtfully provided a choice of two pubs, one in Barrow and the other in nearby Dalton, for those whose thirst needs quenching after their visit to the abbey ruins!

BARROW-IN-FURNESS
Wheatsheaf

Tel: Barrow (0229) 37515
Anson Street (half a mile north of the town centre via Hindpool Road)

✕ lunchtime and evening

John Smith's Bitter

The Wheatsheaf, a building listed for its historical interest, stands in an area of Barrow which once housed a vast dormitory suburb for the nearby iron and steel industry, with countless rows of tenement blocks and terraced houses – most of them, unfortunately, downwind of the blanket of soot and ash from the iron works! All the mills are now closed and many of the old houses have gone, too, though new housing and renovation of the old terraces has given the area a much-needed boost. One feature which has remained unchanged through all this upheaval has been the Wheatsheaf, a classic street-corner local which now as then primarily serves the needs of the local community. The regulars are no longer steelworkers; indeed quite a few of them come from the nearby submarine complex, which explains the mildly nautical theme in the bars. There's an almost old-fashioned feeling (in the nicest possible way) to the pub, with an emphasis in the bar on traditional pub games – hence the popularity of darts, dominoes and shove-ha'-penny at the expense of pool. On the other hand, there *is* rota-pool... but you'll have to ask at the bar for details of that!

BOUTH
White Hart

Tel: Greenodd (022 986) 229
A mile from the A590 at Haverthwaite

✕ lunchtime and evening

Thwaites Best Mild, Bitter

Bouth is a tiny agricultural village (yet one which actually held markets until the early nineteenth century) at the southern end of Grizedale Forest, and indeed the village owes its existence to the former importance of the local woodland industries. The last charcoal burn in the Lake District took place in 1936 at Ealing Hearth, just to the east of the village, and at Haverthwaite the buildings of the Low Wood gunpowder works, which closed in the same year, can still be seen. The White Hart continues the woodland theme with its very varied collection of stuffed animals, the species represented including badger, stoat, weasel and even a hedgehog. There are also stuffed fish and a set of antlers; the pub's dog is, however, decidedly more frisky. The whole interior, with its big fireplace housing an old kitchen range and its mix of wood-panelled and rendered stone walls, is both attractive and relaxing. There are little bow windows set into walls which are four feet thick in places, slabbed stone floors from the Coniston quarries, a beamed ceiling and even a piano. Outside this venerable inn the old "hooker" ring used by coaches that stopped here on their way to London is still attached to the wall. There are a few tables, offering a view across stone-walled fields to the woods above Colton, on a pocket-handkerchief lawn at the back of the pub, and at the front there is another area for summer drinking conveniently within sight of the village playground. On leaving this, one of the nicest pubs in the southern Lake District, there's the chance of a drive northwards up the unspoilt Rusland valley, with views towards the Old Man of Coniston as the road twists and turns between little rock outcrops.

DALTON-IN-FURNESS
Brown Cow

Tel: Dalton (0229) 62553
Goose Green – off A590 on the western outskirts of Dalton

✕ lunchtime and evening

Matthew Brown Bitter; Theakston Best Bitter, XB

The Brown Cow, some of whose timbers are supposed to have been spirited away from Furness Abbey after the Dissolution, is said to be the oldest pub in Dalton, once the capital of Furness but now overshadowed by Barrow. Goose Green though, is hardly part of the town – the terraced cottages and the pub nestle in a sheltered, wooded valley and the prevailing atmosphere hereabouts is that of a sleepy village. The Brown Cow itself oozes hospitality and warmth and is an oasis for lovers of the traditional pub; it's also a regular haunt for denizens of the busy shipbuilding town only a couple of miles to the south-west. Even in the beer garden, though, the illusion of drinking deep in the countryside is sustained, while inside the pub the murmur of good-natured conversation is all that is to be heard – there's a welcome absence of noise pollution from juke boxes or fruit machines. All this is rounded off by excellent bar meals (served downstairs at lunchtime but in the upstairs dining area in the evening) and good beer, so much so that it's difficult for serious drinkers to prise themselves away from the pub to explore Furness Abbey, which is just down the road towards Barrow, or the unspoilt countryside of this somewhat idiosyncratic but strangely attractive peninsula between the Duddon and Leven estuaries.

GREENODD
Ship

Tel: Greenodd (022 986) 304
Main Street

✕ lunchtime and evening

Matthew Brown Mild; Theakston Best Bitter

Greenodd, though it is now simply a quiet village situated on the estuary of the River Crake, was once an important port and shipbuilding centre – indeed, it was to Greenodd that copper ore from Coppermines Valley in the Coniston Fells was sent to be transported to Wales, and the port also handled the Westmorland Dark Blue slates from the Burlington Moor quarry: in 1818 it was reported that "several sloops are constantly employed in the carriage of it from Greenodd to almost every principal seaport town in England and Ireland". The Ship respects this nautical tradition, and locally there is still recognition of the smaller-scale but still vital art of finding a safe passage across the fickle sands of the combined Crake and Leven estuaries (don't take the public footpaths marked on the map too literally – they cross deep water and quicksands!). Behind the bar a cryptic notice informs customers that "The last liberty boat leaves for shore at ten-thirty pm", while around the walls there is a wide variety of maps and nautical charts together with ships' photographs. The large lounge bar is pleasant enough, though the pool table is placed so as to dominate most of it, and the bar food, despite a fairly standard selection of dishes, is generously proportioned and appetising.

GRIZEBECK
Greyhound Inn

Tel: Kirkby-in-Furness (022 989) 224
On A595

✕ lunchtime (weekends only) and evening

John Smith Bitter

The Greyhound is a 200 year-old roadside inn, part of a hamlet nestling below the extensive spoil heaps of the Burlington Slate Quarry on Kirkby Fell (the spoil heaps make an unusually evocative picture when viewed in low light from the slopes around Bank End to the west). The quarry, the largest in England and famous throughout the world for its Westmorland Dark Blue slates, so-called even though the quarry was then in Lancashire, is the successor to the tiny quarries hacked out by local farmers in the eighteenth century, and is one of only half a dozen existing in the National Park today. The quarry also supplied the slate floors of the inn, while the oak bar top was fashioned from local timber which was unseasoned and as a result is now far from straight (the landlord is counting on a few years of sustained handpump-pulling to correct this deformity!). Very popular at the weekends for its generous, good-value bar meals, the Greyhound also has a separate games room for those wanting nothing more than to relax over a game of darts, dominoes or don, and a very pleasant garden. There's an outstandingly friendly welcome and a sense of unhurried well-being – but not on weekday lunchtimes, when the pub (even after the advent of the new licensing laws) is likely to remain closed. It's very well worth a visit at all other times, however.

LOWICK
Farmers Arms

Tel: Ulverston (0229) 86277
On A593 at Lowick Green

- lunchtime and evening
- Younger No. 3

Although the Farmers Arms was originally a farmhouse – and the typically long, low buildings of a Cumbrian farmstead survive, though now only as part of a much larger complex – the owners long ago turned their hand to brewing ale for travellers. Sadly home-brewed beer is no longer available, but this attractive, traditional Lakeland hostelry now has something for everyone, though many will find most interest in the public bar, with its flagstoned floor and tudor-style beams, its old oak settles and its little enclosed areas offering the chance of a quiet drink. There is also a variety of traditional pub games and, strangely, a *papier-maché* horse's head. The lounge is comfortable and notable for its display of interesting local photographs – though you will have to carry your real ale through from the Stable Bar. Outside there are tables dotted around for summer drinking. The bar food is good, varied and filling, and includes Stilton paté, potted shrimps and an excellent steak, kidney and stout pie. For those with deeper pockets and even bigger appetites there is a separate restaurant. The accommodation, along stone-flagged passages and across the courtyard, is pleasantly unassuming; there is more in a converted barn which has been incorporated into the inn.

Red Lion

Tel: Lowick Bridge (022 985) 366
Just off A5084 at Lowick Bridge

- lunchtime and evening
- Hartley Mild, Fellrunners, XB

Beautifully situated in rolling countryside, the Red Lion is a warmly welcoming, traditional country inn with excellent beer from nearby Ulverston and a well-deserved reputation for good food. The pub lies within yards of the main road at Lowick Bridge – there is little else in the hamlet apart from the buildings of a former watermill down by the attractive stone bridge over the River Crake, here only a mile or so downstream from the lower end of Coniston Water – and it is very easily found, especially at night when it can be identified by its somewhat garish pink floodlighting. From several points close by there is a wonderful panorama of the Coniston Fells, and all of the southern lakes and mountains are within very easy reach. At nearby Nibthwaite the forge oven of a long-defunct iron furnace survives. Inside the Red Lion there is a relaxed atmosphere in the two comfortable rooms, and it is no coincidence that the pub is very well patronised by the local farming community, not least at the time of the Lowick Agricultural Show in early September. The regulars tend to congregate particularly in the bar, with its unfussy decoration and variety of pub games. And for tourists needing a bed for the night, the accommodation is also pleasantly furnished and offers good value.

OXEN PARK
Manor House

Tel: Greenodd (022 986) 345
Two miles east of A5084 at Lowick Bridge, OS318873

- lunchtime and evening
- Hartley's Mild, Fellrunners, XB

The Manor House really is just that – a converted former manor house which became a pub in the nineteen-thirties and, largely in response to a severe case of dry rot, has recently been very considerably and thoughtfully renovated. There is now a very large lounge bar, airy and spacious with a high beamed ceiling, and a smaller side room. Outside there is a stylish raised patio with several tables and tubs of flowers at the front, and very attractively landscaped lawns and car park at the side and rear. Happily the Manor House manages to combine the roles of village local and provider of sustenance to hungry (and thirsty) tourists. There are pub games and regular folk nights together with excellent beer, and good home-made food, ranging from a bowl of soup to a varied *à la carte* menu. All this happens in a pub situated in a relatively remote hamlet – though one on a good road which heads up through Grizedale Forest, between Coniston Water and Lake Windermere, and eventually reaches Hawkshead. Oxen Park, which takes its name from its medieval location at the centre of the oxen-grazing grounds of Furness Abbey, whose vast landholdings were concentrated in this area of low hills, is now a peaceful but quite attractive agricultural hamlet close to the much-visited church at Colton.

SPARK BRIDGE
Royal Oak

Tel: Greenodd (022 986) 286
Within half a mile of A590 at Lowick Green

✕ lunchtime and evening

Thwaites Best Mild, Bitter

A traditional country pub which is clearly extremely popular for its very wide selection of bar meals, the Royal Oak lies right in the middle of the little village of Spark Bridge. There is a very pleasant little saloon bar at the back for traditionalists, with a dartboard squeezed somewhat improbably into a corner, a collection of water jugs above the bar counter and an instructive framed poster headed "Articles for a Cock Match". The real heart of the pub, though, is the main lounge bar, which spreads impressively around the rest of the ground floor and is largely given over to eating, though there is a pool table at the far end. There is also an upstairs bar which is very popular for Sunday lunches. The food includes local trout, Cumberland sausage, duckling, game pie, a wide selection of salads and an astonishing variety of sweets, including "death by chocolate cake". In the winter there are open log fires, and live music is a further attraction on Friday nights. At the rear of the pub a nice, comparatively quiet beer garden runs down towards the banks of the River Crake, on the far side of which are the dilapidated but still fascinating remains of the last bobbin mill to close in the Lake District. Now it is necessary to travel to nearby Low Stott Park, above the southern reaches of Windermere, to see (restored as a working museum) a "living" example of this most common of Lakeland woodland industries, developed to serve the textile industries of Yorkshire and Lancashire but destroyed by cheap imports and the development of plastic bobbins.

ULVERSTON
Devonshire Arms

Tel: Ulverston (0229) 52537
Victoria Road

- ✕ lunchtime
- ◎ at lunchtime
- Thwaites Best Mild, Bitter

This is in many ways a typical Victorian suburban pub, a solid and prosperous-looking building a short walk from the town centre and within easy reach of the bus and railway stations. Formerly owned by Case's of the Cavendish Brewery in Barrow (which ceased brewing in 1972), this, together with the Horse & Groom in Market Street, is one of the furthest-flung Thwaites' pubs and provides a welcome alternative to Hartley's, Ulverston's own brew. There's a guarantee of a very friendly welcome in either of the two bars. The public bar is fairly straightforward, functional rather than opulent but exactly suited to the needs of its remarkably varied clientele. Particularly noteworthy is the heavy emphasis on pub games and an almost fanatical interest in the local Sunday quiz league. The lounge, approached through a little glass porch, attracts all age groups and is consequently very popular and often quite crowded. The many pictures of aircraft which decorate the walls (and thereby provide welcome relief from the horse brasses and flying ducks of so many Lakeland pubs) result from the landlord's own very strong interest in the subject. The pub attracts discerning drinkers from afar: try the award-winning mild to see why.

Globe

Tel: Ulverston (0229) 53416
Queen Street

- ✕ lunchtime
- Hartley Bitter, Fellrunners, XB

One of a whole host of pubs in the relatively small town centre of Ulverston – the King's Head is right next door and the Rose & Crown only a few steps away! – the Globe stands out not because of its external appearance, which is relatively unassuming, but because of its distinctively remodelled and renovated interior and its traditional Cumbrian welcome. The single bar, thoughtfully decorated largely in subdued shades of blue, is a popular venue for a quiet drink in civilised surroundings (though like most Ulverston pubs the Globe can become very heavily populated on Friday and Saturday evenings). The bench seating, together with bar stools and low tables, is arranged around a U-shaped bar, itself propped up on a regular basis by groups of locals. The food is slightly disappointing: a rather more adventurous choice of dishes would not go amiss. But this is a pleasant watering-hole, full of nice touches such as the bowls of flowers in strategic corners, and it's an extremely convenient diversion for those attending the weekly markets or for tourists and shoppers strolling around the food stalls in Market Street.

King's Head

Tel: Ulverston (0229) 56325
Queen Street

- ✕ lunchtime
- ❀
- 🛏
- **Theakston Best Bitter; regular guest beers**

A premier venue for Ulverston pubgoers, the King's Head gets even more crowded than the other pubs featured in this book, and it's highly desirable to get there early to claim a table for a bar lunch or for an evening drink. Some 300 years old, it is low-ceilinged and oak-beamed, and is particularly welcoming in winter, when there are blazing log fires to warm customers on the coldest day. The food, though, is restricted to snacks and bar meals at lunchtime, and it's the beer, including some interesting guest beers, which attracts much of the custom. At the rear there is a terrace and a beautifully kept beer garden for summer drinking, and beyond this a surprisingly large crown bowling green (woods for hire at the bar). The King's Head has always kept its doors open all day on Thursday, market day in Ulverston, and undoubtedly this is a good time to visit, with lots of cheery local banter and a certain amount of horse-trading going on in the comfortable bar. This is an interesting place to stay, too, right in the centre of Ulverston yet still close to High Furness and the southern fells around Coniston.

Rose and Crown

Tel: Ulverston (0229) 53094
King Street

✕ lunchtime and evening

Hartley Mild, Fellrunners, XB

This is a delightful town pub, bursting with character, which has undergone a recent sympathetic renovation and now makes a splendid contribution to the drinking scene in Ulverston. Inside there is a mixture of styles, with a black-and-white motif fairly widespread but some exposed stonework too. The uneven stone floors testify to the age of the inn, which dates from 1654, and there are also a number of distinctive drinking areas, including a wonderful little snug which was formerly the pantry bar. The central serving area caters for this and a variety of other rooms and odd corners, none of them in any way plush but all in keeping with the character of the place. The locals appreciate it this way too, for this vibrant pub is highly popular in Ulverston, especially at weekends and also on Wednesdays, when there is a regular folk night. It's quite a well-known eating spot at lunchtime, too, with an extensive list of bar meals on offer. There's a sense of history in the air at the pub: for example, ask the landlord about the story of Jamie Kelly's chair... One slight quibble is with the music, which is intrusively loud at times and difficult to escape from, that apart, the Rose and Crown is an essential halting place on the drinker's tour of the best pubs in the Lake District.

Spectacular mountain scenery, a classically long and narrow lake, and a host of other tourist attractions ranging from historic houses through market towns to ancient monuments such as stone circles – no wonder this area is regarded with affection by so many. And there is a remarkable range of good pubs in which to round off a memorable day's walking or sight-seeing!

The mountains are the Coniston Fells, of which the highest (but only just) is the Old Man of Coniston, not a place on which you are ever likely to feel lonely given its huge popularity. The Old Man towers above the village of Coniston and the tourist route to its summit lies through Coppermines Valley, a fascinating area of industrial dereliction which is well worth exploring for its own sake. Other notable summits in this group of fells include Wetherlam, pockmarked with quarries but a pleasant walk, and Grey Friar, notable for its magnificent prospect over the Scafell range.

Two lakes dominate the area: quiet, sylvan Esthwaite Water and the much more dramatic Coniston Water, notorious as the site of Donald Campbell's attempt on the world water-speed record in 1967 but now equally notable as the home of the Gondola, a steamboat once again in regular service after years of neglect as a forlorn wreck at the southern end of the lake. The mountain scenery from the eastern shore of the lake is superlative. Just as good, though, is Dunnerdale, the valley of the River Duddon; here there is no lake but spectacularly glorious scenery, with towering crags, rough fell country and peaceful woods together with a river running through little gorges and over stepping stones around the exquisite farming hamlet of Seathwaite.

On the eastern shores of Coniston Water is Brantwood, former home of the writer, painter and philosopher John Ruskin; in nearby Coniston the Ruskin Museum is small but full of intriguing material. Further east is Beatrix Potter's home at Hill Top Farm in Near Sawrey, inspiration for the "Peter Rabbit" series of books. And Hawkshead, an interesting little place in its own right, has Wordsworth's grammar school, with the original desks and benches, and the whole building preserved much as the poet would have known it.

The towns and villages include, in addition to Hawkshead and Coniston, the market centre of Broughton, well worth a visit on market day (Tuesday). As for the ancient monuments, they include the Swinside stone circle, high up on the eastern flanks of Black Combe but rewarding the enterprising tourist with not only a close-up view of perhaps the best of the Lake District's few neolithic stone circles, with some 55 stones still in position, but also an excellent view southwards to the wide expanse of the Duddon Sands. Little Arrow Moor, west of Coniston, has its stone circles too, though these are more difficult to find. The Walna Scar Road, originating as a prehistoric trackway threading its way across the moor on its way to Seathwaite in Dunnerdale (and the exceptionally hospitable Newfield Inn) is more accessible and well worth walking for the high quality mountain scenery it reveals.

BARNGATES
Drunken Duck

Tel: Hawkshead (096 66) 347
Three miles south west of Ambleside, off B5286. OS351052

✕ lunchtime and evening

Jennings Bitter; Marston Pedigree; Theakston XB, Old Peculier; Tetley Bitter; regular guest beers

Slightly off the beaten track but still close to Coniston, Ambleside and the (very) popular National Trust beauty spot of Tarn Hows, the Drunken Duck stands at a minor crossroads west of Outgate and has a pleasant prospect over distant fells. Residents are especially fortunate here: they have the use of two local trout tarns. But non-residents are almost as well catered for, with appealing food (including mouth-watering desserts), a splendid range of real draught beer and an even more formidable array of malt whiskies to choose from. There is a long narrow bar decorated with an assortment of hunting trophies, including foxes' heads, together with brasses and pewter mugs. Families and diners can use either of the two excellent side rooms, while at the side of the pub there is a patio and beer garden. The inn, dating from the sixteenth century, was once known as the Barngates Inn, but assumed its present name in Victorian times after, so the doubtless much-embellished story goes, the landlady discovered half-a-dozen inebriated ducks lying in the road. Assuming that they were dead, she plucked them; but when they suddenly began to show signs of life she realized they had been sampling the contents of a leaking cask of beer. Legend has it that she knitted them woollen jackets to wear until their feathers grew again. Believe that if you will; but the present pub needs no such tales to attract customers from far and wide.

BROUGHTON IN FURNESS
Black Cock Inn

Tel: Broughton (065 76) 529
Princess Street.

✕ lunchtime and evening

Webster Yorkshire Bitter, Choice; Ruddles County

Broughton might not appear to be a particularly obvious choice as a base for a holiday in the southern Lake District, yet in fact it is superbly situated close to Coniston Water and Dunnerdale, and is a fascinating little charter town in its own right, bursting into life on Tuesdays when the farmers flock in to the busy livestock market. The market was established in the late seventeenth century, and the spacious market place laid out on land provided by John Gilpin (who is commemorated by an obelisk) a hundred years later. The Black Cock, which originated in the sixteenth century as a coaching inn, reflects this combination of history and bustling activity – it has always stayed open all day on market days as a service to the farming community – and now comprises a comfortable dining room and a low-beamed lounge exuding charm and tranquility. The former stables have been converted to form a lively games room. There is also a garden at the rear of the pub. It's a particularly attractive, whitewashed town pub, with the sills and lintels boldly picked out in black, and window boxes and hanging baskets relieving the somewhat stark effect of the colour scheme. The rather extraordinary pub sign is dominated by an outsize black cock. The food is tasty and includes an excellent prawn salad and venison pie; a take-away food service is available. It's an ideal place to stay, too, with a selection of good-value twin-bedded, double and family rooms.

One dog and his man

Old King's Head

Tel: Broughton (065 76) 293
Station Road

- ✕ lunchtime and evening
- ☺
- 🛏
- Hartley XB; Whitbread guest beers

This is a really popular market town pub, vibrant and cheerful: a fine touring base but equally inviting as a venue for a quick pint of Hartley's or a bar meal. The simple but tasty meals are popular not just with summer tourists but all year round with the locals: a singular but well-deserved recommendation! It's a typically long, low whitewashed building tucked away slightly from the centre of Broughton, with a solitary table to one side of the main doorway. Inside, low oak beams and unfussy decoration retain the original character, with a very long lounge bar split into three distinct sections – one dominated by the inevitable pool table – and a separate and extremely popular dining room through an archway to the left. Broughton remains very much a centre for the local farming community – all the more so since the trade brought by the woodland and woollen industries around the town has dried up. The Old King's Head functions admirably in its dual role as watering hole for the locals and welcoming inn for tourists who are slightly more adventurous than usual, at least in terms of straying from the main tourist sights. It's a hive of activity at all times, with a general buzz of conversation characterising the bars, and it pays to get there early in the evening to claim a seat.

CONISTON
Crown

Tel: Coniston (0966) 41243
Off A593

- ✕ lunchtime and evening
- ❀
- ☺
- 🛏
- Hartley Mild, Fellrunners, XB; Robinson Old Tom

This is a typical Lakes village pub, squat and whitewashed, and very conveniently placed for the centre of the village. The heart of the pub is the comfortable old public bar, with low lighting, weatherbeaten chairs and tables (and indeed weatherbeaten locals at many of them), a roaring log fire in winter and the specially warming sight of a cask of Old Tom, Robinson's magnificent draught barley wine, on the counter. The Crown also has a rather more subdued lounge bar, with distinctly less character, and a dining room where family parties are welcome. Less than welcome, though, are motorcyclists! The building lies behind a big car park, part of which (protected by a low wall) has been furnished with tables and chairs to function as a beer "garden" which is actually quite a suntrap. The pub can get very busy at peak times, a tribute to the pulling power of Hartley's – and Coniston itself. It's quite a nice place to stay, though the accommodation is perhaps a little old-fashioned. The Crown lies between the Old Man of Coniston and the lake, with easy access to both, and it is only a short stroll from Coppermines Valley (worth visiting for the views even if you don't find industrial archaeology too gripping) and from the Ruskin Museum in the village.

Ship Inn

Tel: Coniston (0966) 41224
At Bowmanstead, one mile south of Coniston on A593

✕ available lunchtime and evening

Hartley XB; Robinson Old Tom

Compact and friendly, the Ship is a tremendous find. It's a surprisingly adventurous pub tucked away above, and easily missed from, the main road running between Coniston and Broughton. Travelling from Coniston, if you see Bowmanstead's slate-grey church tower to your right, you've missed it! The approach, up a steep lane between cottages and a gaunt barn, is unpromising but this belies the convivial atmosphere inside, with unpretentious but comfortable seating in a partly-beamed bar boasting a big, solid stone fireplace. A notable feature is the enormous bell suspended above the bar – this is one pub where the customers know when it's time to go! A side room has music and pub games. In front of the pub, on a rather homemade patio, there are a few rustic tables and benches. The XB is a treat and, as with the Crown in the centre of Coniston, there is also the fearsome Old Tom for the brave (or foolhardy). Amongst the interesting items on offer for the famished are game pie and, intriguingly, crab and vegetable parcels in a sweet and sour sauce. After the food and drink serious walkers will no doubt be tempted by the signpost, literally in the front yard of the pub, advertising the scenic walk over Little Arrow Moor, joining the ancient Walna Scar Road (now a green track) on its way to Seathwaite in Dunnerdale.

Yewdale Hotel

Tel: Coniston (0966) 41280
Yewdale Road (junction of A593 and B5285).

✕ lunchtime and evening

Hartley XB; Whitbread Castle Eden Ale

Opposite the church in the centre of Coniston, the Yewdale is a pleasant, relaxed hotel offering good food and beer. It's an imposing building, fashioned from local stone and slate, on a corner site, and it's surprising that it dates only from 1896. Originally it was partly a bank and partly a guest house, and it has been very well converted to form the present intimate hotel, with six letting bedrooms including two family rooms. The old bank now forms the lounge bar of the hotel, and its interest and indeed attractiveness is much enhanced by the retention of the original oak woodwork, including the bank's oak counter. Subtly decorated with a lot of pink furnishings, the Yewdale is a nice spot to relax away from the bustle of Coniston's village centre and lake shore. There's also a very extensive selection of meals, served in the lounge bar or in the separate dining room, with a long list of steaks; other specialities include honey-baked ham and, perhaps for late risers, rambler's brunch. There is a varied children's menu too. A popular excursion, only ten minutes walk away is a trip on Coniston Water, on the luxury steamboat "Gondola", recently restored by the National Trust. Tarn Hows is just one of the beauty spots nearby; quieter but just as rewarding is the Tilberthwaite valley, with an old spinning gallery at Yew Tree Farm and delightful waterfalls higher up.

FAR SAWREY
Sawrey Hotel

Tel: Windermere (096 62) 3425/4651
On B5285

- ✕ lunchtime and evening
-
-
-
- **Theakston Best Bitter, XB, Old Peculier**

The Sawrey Hotel is an elegant eighteenth-century hotel close to the western shore of Lake Windermere. A regular and surprisingly inexpensive vehicle ferry connects Sawrey with the eastern shore near the tourist haunts of Bowness and Windermere town, so the area is not quite as secluded as one might expect, but it is easy to escape into the low fells around the village, and especially the wooded, tarn-studded Claife Heights, which offers simple walking but very extensive views of lakes and mountains. Hill Top Farm, where Beatrix Potter wrote and illustrated the "Peter Rabbit" series of children's books, is not very far away, and both Hawkshead and Grizedale Forest are within a few minutes' drive. The Sawrey Hotel has a fascinating public bar, the Claife Crier (named after a character who supposedly lured boatmen and their passengers on the old ferry to their deaths in misty weather). The bar is situated in the converted stables of the hotel, with seating in the former stalls, and harnesses and other equestrian gear decorating the walls. There are also very comfortable lounges and, perhaps best of all when the somewhat erratic Lake District weather is at its best, a marvellously situated terrace with spectacular views of the lake. This is a wonderful spot to sit, with a glass of Theakston's in hand, and perhaps a bar meal from the reasonable choice on offer, while craft of all description throng the waters of Windermere below.

HAWKSHEAD
King's Arms

Tel: Hawkshead (096 66) 372
The Square

✕ lunchtime and evening

Matthew Brown Mild; Theakston Best Bitter; Tetley Bitter

There is a large pay-and-display car park close to the centre of Hawkshead, and judging by the sheer weight of numbers in the town's streets on a typical summer's day it seems reasonable to suppose that the local council makes a fair profit from it. It's easy to understand why the tourists come, however: not only is there the undoubted attraction of Wordsworth's grammar school, there is a substantial wool church, with a stupendous view of distant fells from the churchyard, and a series of cobbled lanes, courtyards and squares overhung in some cases by houses dating from the great rebuilding of the early seventeenth century. The King's Arms, a cottagey building with an archway to the right, overlooks the square and contributes to its richly attractive environment. There's a pleasant small garden behind a low wall, and inside the pub the low-beamed bar is decorated with prints, many of them showing local scenes. There's another room off to the right, and a separate restaurant; the bar food ranges from sandwiches to full meals including a good vegetarian risotto. The accommodation, in the hotel itself and in a nearby cottage, is attractive and reasonably priced – the winter breaks in particular are temptingly good value.

Queen's Head

Tel: Hawkshead (096 66) 271
Main Street

✕ lunchtime and evening

Hartley Mild, Fellrunners, XB; Robinson Old Tom

A splendid, hospitable inn with a heavy emphasis on food – the menu is, by the standards of most Lake District pubs, startlingly original. The Queen's Head is a spectacularly busy pub, virtually bursting at the seams at the height of the tourist season. Partly this is due to its position, right in the middle of Hawkshead and conveniently placed for the main tourist sights, but the food and beer has a fine reputation too. Its Elizabethan look is a little contrived – those black-and-white beams are painted on the exterior – but it can trace its origins to the seventeenth century and the beamed bar is full of authentic character. In addition to comfortable accommodation the inn offers bar meals at all times. A really good *à la carte* menu served in the splendid surroundings of an oak-panelled dining room includes such delicacies as roast guinea fowl, fillet of Esthwaite trout, chicken *cacciatora* and jugged hare. The trout is a reminder of the nearness of Esthwaite Water, perhaps the least known of the Lake District's major lakes but nevertheless attractive in its own gentle way. There's an excellent prospect over the reedy, tree-fringed lake to the Langdale Pikes, and at Esthwaite North Fen (Priest Pot) there is a National Nature Reserve.

NEAR SAWREY
Tower Bank Arms

Tel: Hawkshead (096 66) 334
On B5288.

- ✕ lunchtime and evening
- **Matthew Brown Mild; Theakston Best Bitter, XB; Younger Scotch, No. 3**

The National Trust owns and runs the Tower Bank Arms, a small but delightful pub virtually next to Hill Top Farm, once the home of Beatrix Potter. Not only did she make extensive use of the surrounding countryside as settings for her "Peter Rabbit" stories, she used the pub itself, and indeed it is still instantly recognisable from the illustration in "The Tale of Jemima Puddle-duck" – though the hand-drawn butcher's cart she portrayed in front of the pub is no longer there! In front of the black-and-white cottage style pub there are a few tables for summer days, while inside there is an informal, friendly atmosphere, with a good selection of real ales and an equally wide range of tempting, reasonably-priced bar food. The bar is traditional, indeed almost austere, with flagged floors and high-backed pew-style seating, but there is a roaring fire in winter and a general bustle of activity. The dining room at the side is simple but attractive; families are welcome to use it. Hill Top Farm, a typical seventeenth-century farmhouse which is now the most visited house in the Lake District *despite* the National Trust's attempts to staunch the flow of tourists, is worth the visit for its unpretentious but carefully preserved interior. Also worthy of note are the local footpaths, especially the track leading northwards and winding between a series of little tarns on Claife Heights: this is the southern Lake District at its most picturesque.

OUTGATE
Outgate Inn

Tel: Hawkshead (096 66) 413
On B5286 three miles south-west of Ambleside

✕ lunchtime and evening

Hartley Mild, Fellrunners, XB; Robinson Old Tom

This is a popular venue for tourists in the southern Lake District, and as a result the small, awkward car park and the surrounding verges are often packed with cars during the season. What they come for is the Hartley's beer and especially the bar meals, which are served at all times and, whilst they are not particularly unusual, are well-presented and nourishing. There is a big main bar, with the bar counter oddly angled across it and tables, chairs and bar stools at some distance from the counter – wisely so for this area becomes crowded with groups of drinkers standing up and enjoying a "crack" as the evening wears on. A comfortable side room is available for (well-behaved) children at lunchtime and in the early evening; and an overflow area, with yet more seating but rather plainer surroundings, is situated to the left of the entrance. A particular attraction for some will be the absence of intrusive music – there is no juke box. The Outgate is a useful place to know for those who need to stay overnight in this area; for tourists with time to spare it's very close to Ambleside and Hawkshead, and closer still to the noted beauty spot of Tarn Hows, with its splendid panoramic views of the Langdale Pikes and the Helvellyn range. There are some excellent local walks, too, none better than the footpath starting just north of the hamlet of Outgate and leading down past Blelham Tarn to the imposing fake-medieval Wray Castle (actually built in the 1840s).

SEATHWAITE
Newfield Inn

Tel: Broughton (065 76) 208
In the village of Seathwaite in upper Dunnerdale. OS228959

- available lunchtime and evening
- self-catering flats
- **Younger Scotch Bitter**

The Newfield Inn, located in a tiny farming hamlet right in the heart of unspoilt Dunnerdale, is a magnificent example of an unchanging dales pub. Catering throughout the year for the locals, it also lays on a tremendous welcome for summer visitors, and is well-known for its food, especially steaks – at very reasonable prices – served in either the dining room (a haven for non-smokers) or in the wonderful old bar. The slate floor of the bar originates from the long-disused Walna Scar quarry (close to the Walna Scar Road, an ancient trackway over Little Arrow Moor to Coniston) and clearly shows the layers of volcanic dust which formed underwater sediments: each stripe represents a different eruption. There are no volcanoes in Dunnerdale now, but the whole area is magnificent fell-walking country, with the marvellous Harter Fell dominating the upper valley and the long ridge of the Coniston Fells filling the skyline to the east, beyond Seathwaite Tarn in its green bowl below Grey Friar. At a lower level there are also pleasant walks along the banks of the River Duddon, both close to the village and also further upstream, around the much-photographed Birks Bridge, a high packhorse bridge spanning the river as it runs through a little rocky gorge.

SILECROFT
Miners Arms

Tel: Millom (0657) 2325
Off A595 near Silecroft station

- lunchtime and evening
- **Younger Scotch Bitter, No. 3**

There are two very different reasons for this pub standing out in the memory of visitors. The first is the giant whaleback of Black Combe, the most southerly serious fell of the Lake District, its rounded green slopes, composed of an outlier of Skiddaw Slates, dominating the village. On the far side is the Swinside stone circle, well worth finding along narrow lanes and then a farm track. The second is the highly unusual and definitely memorable tradition of giving a glass of home-made mulled ale to all visitors on Easter

Sunday evening. The Miners Arms is a seventeenth-century coaching inn, very well renovated and now offering comfortable accommodation – both for overnight guests and for those simply dropping in for a pint. Silecroft, hard to reach at the south-west tip of the National Park, is full of interest, boasting a horse-ginn (a roughcast building where a mule or donkey attached to a beam walked round in a circle, turning a pair of rollers to crush corn, oats or barley), a former Hall now converted into a row of cottages, one of which enjoys the name "Breeches Arse Cottage", and Arrow Hill, part of a natural dam which penned back a huge lake in glacial times.

The three dales of Eskdale, Wasdale and Ennerdale offer, in the opinion of many, the finest and most spectacular mountain scenery, together with a sense of peace and quiet which is altogether missing in some of the more popular central valleys. Together with the surprisingly attractive western coast – especially at Ravenglass, where three rivers join to flow as one into the Irish Sea, and at St. Bees, where the village nestles beneath sandstone cliffs – they form an area of often dramatic and never less than interesting scenery.

Eskdale has no lake – though in the Ice Ages there was more than one – but in all other respects is quite superb. At the remote head of the dale are the highest mountains in England, and the most rewarding climb to their summits starts here. Lower down, at Boot, there are two fine inns as well as marvellous stretches of riverside walking, a spectacular waterfall, and a restored watermill. Lower again, there are attractions as varied as the miniature-gauge Ravenglass and Eskdale railway, the splendour of the gardens at Muncaster Castle, the Roman bath-house at Walls Castle, and the estuary at Ravenglass, with the Drigg Dunes nature reserve across the water. Wasdale is the most dramatic of all, with the brooding Screes cascading down from the summits of Illgill Head and Whin Rigg to the magnificent Wastwater, the deepest lake and one hemmed in at its head by a ring of grand mountains – Scafell Pike, the highest of them all, Lingmell, Great Gable (symbol of the National Park) and Yewbarrow. But there are treasures on a more human scale too, such as the delightful packhorse bridge and tiny church at Wasdale Head; the wonderfully-situated inn, an historic spot for rock-climbers, in the dalehead hamlet; and the tall, slender Viking cross and hogback tombstones at Gosforth.

Ennerdale, the most northerly of the three, is

perhaps the least well-known, though this is more because of the efforts of the Forestry Commission than because of any demerits in the scenery itself. The green blanket of conifers which has for so long clothed the lower valley has been reduced by clear-felling (but replanting will soon make up for that), but the majestic outline of Pillar Rock still soars above the trees, and at the dalehead the extraordinarily isolated Black Sail youth hostel still stands below mountains such as Haystacks and Great Gable. Access up the dale is still very restricted, and the quiet little village of Ennerdale Bridge is the limit for most travellers; lower down the River Ehen the town of Egremont, overlooked by a ruined castle, is worth a look, as is Whitehaven, a Georgian planned town with a grid-iron street pattern.

BECKERMET
Royal Oak

Tel: Beckermet (094 684) 551
Half a mile west of A595

✕ lunchtime and evening

Jennings Bitter

This is a notably friendly pub, one of the most important centres of the community in a mostly residential village which is actually only just off the A595 south of Egremont, but which somehow has a sense of being rather further off the beaten track. It is, however, very close to the nuclear works at Sellafield, and is popular with employees from there, as well as with visitors to that most unlikely of fast-growing tourist attractions. Formerly a well-respected free house, it has now been taken into the Jennings' fold, but it is in all other respects unchanged, with a central serving counter and a plethora of small self-contained drinking areas. The furnishings are somewhat spartan, with quarry-tiled floors and solid wooden tables, but the bar snacks, available all day, are tasty and very filling. To one side of the main drinking area is a fully-fledged games room. From several points in and around the village there are wide-ranging views of the rounded, grassy fells forming a mass of remote and seldom visited high ground between Ennerdale and Wasdale, while for the truly adventurous the seashore at Nethertown and Braystones is close at hand.

BOOT
Burnmoor Inn

Tel: Eskdale (094 03) 224
Just off the valley road in the hamlet of Boot, seven miles east of Holmrook

✕ lunchtime and evening

Jennings Bitter

Tony and Heidi Foster run a wonderful little hotel here, with real ale, good food and splendid accommodation in an idyllic part of the Lake District. At the bottom of the lane on the opposite side of the main valley road is St. Catherine's chapel and, nearby, stepping stones across the River Esk. Even closer to the Burnmoor are the painstakingly preserved cornmill with its working waterwheel, and a packhorse bridge over the Whillan Beck at the start of the Old Corpse Road over which the dead were once brought from Wasdale Head past the wild and lonely Burnmoor Tarn to Boot for burial. The whitewashed, partly seventeenth-century hotel has low fells rising up immediately behind it, and is tucked away off the valley road. Now very well maintained, it is hardly recognisable as the very simple country inn it in fact was until a short time ago. It is, however, well worth seeking out for its safe, walled and fenced garden, its attractive and welcoming bar, and its food, served in either the bar or the restaurant, which occupies the former stables. There's a high-quality mixture of local and Austrian dishes ranging from Cumberland game pie to *Wiener-schnitzel*. There is also a children's menu, and a good pint of Cumbrian bitter from the hand-pump.

Woolpack

Tel: Eskdale (094 03) 230
On the valley road a mile east of Boot and eight miles east of Holmrook

✕ lunchtime and evening

Younger IPA

The Woolpack Inn was built, as its name suggests, to serve the packhorse trains using the notorious Hardknott Pass, the only route east-wards out of Eskdale. Ironically the packhorse trade which had prompted its construction began to decline soon after the inn was opened, and it is fortunate that the modern tourist trade has provided the old inn with a new *raison d'être*. In the days before the Woolpack there was another inn, the Pyet's Nest, at Penny Hill farm on the opposite side of the valley. Now the tourists pour past on their way to Brotherilkeld, below the Roman fort of Hardknott, and then the tortuous, steep Hardknott Pass itself. Most live to tell the tale of their crossing, but not every car escapes unscathed and it is worth avoiding Hardknott during peak times! The Woolpack, an attractive pair of linked white-painted buildings set back from the road, is the ideal place to relax after the horrors of Hardknott, with a comfort-able bar ideal for walkers, a rather more salubrious lounge and a very pleasant beer garden in front of the pub. The garden has fine views across the valley to Harter Fell – a particularly majestic mountain from this angle.

The Woolpack places great emphasis on friendly, efficient service. It offers morning coffee, bar lunches and excellent dinners in a separate restaurant.

CALDERBRIDGE
Stanley Arms Hotel

Tel: Beckermet (094 684) 235
On A595

✕ lunchtime and evening

Younger Scotch

A typical small Cumbrian hotel in a hamlet on the main coast road, close to the Sellafield works. The lounge bar is an exceptionally nice place to spend a little time, with plenty of space, plush seating and lots of wood panelling. Even nicer, perhaps, are the gardens behind and below the hotel. There are a number of picnic tables in this delightfully peaceful spot overlooking the fast-flowing River Calder – noted for its sea trout and salmon – in its rocky bed. Residents have the special perk of fishing rights, with a reasonable chance of success in one of the river's deep pools. A good variety of food is available, served lunchtime and evening in both the lounge bar and the restaurant. Families are welcome in these rooms or in the wide entrance hall. Both Eskdale and Wasdale are within easy reach of the Stanley Arms, so that the Ravenglass and Eskdale railway and the spectacular mountains around Wasdale Head can quickly be visited, but perhaps the most evocative outing is that along the fell road to Ennerdale. This quite narrow but well-surfaced road leaves the A595 in the hamlet, passes the ruins of Calder Abbey, and runs through wild fell country, offering wide views into the remote and seldom visited far western fells, then skirts the Kinniside stone circle on its way to Ennerdale Bridge.

Enjoying a pint of mild

EGREMONT
Blue Bell

Tel: Egremont (0946) 820581
Market Place

✕ lunchtime

Hartley XB

A neatly modernised one-roomed town local, the Blue Bell is popular with a good cross-section of the community, including the younger set. There certainly seems to be more characters per square inch in this typically friendly little pub than in most others in the Lakes! The Blue Bell has strong rugby league connections, and there are plenty of rugby photographs around the walls. There are few frills, but this delightfully uncomplicated boozer serves excellent beer and has in its time collected a host of devotees. Salmon fishing permits are available behind the bar, and the locals will advise on the right stretches of the River Ehen to try. The pub is right on the main street, opposite the war memorial, and is therefore well situated for the festivities connected with the Egremont Crab Fair in September – one of the best local events in Cumbria, though it tends to be somewhat overshadowed now by the "World Championship Gurning Competition" held at the same time. Egremont is a town of some historical distinction, with a weekly market which has been held since 1267, and the remains of a Norman castle overlooking the Ehen at the south end of the town centre. The castle is connected with the legend of the Horn of Egremont, which inspired William Wordsworth to write, in 1806, of: "The Horn of Egremont Castle...which none could sound...save he who came as rightful heir".

The pub cat

ESKDALE GREEN
Bower House

Tel: Eskdale (094 03) 244
On the valley road four miles east of Holmrook

✕ lunchtime and evening

Hartley XB; Theakston Best Bitter; Younger Scotch

The royal way to arrive at this pub is by train – one of the halts on the Ravenglass and Eskdale miniature railway is only a short stroll away. The Bower House is situated in a superbly scenic setting, in a scattered village which is home to the Eskdale Outward Bound Mountain School and is close to some of the highest and best mountains in England. It's a cosy country inn of great character, dating from the seventeenth century, and features of the main lounge bar include oak beams, nice wooden chairs and sporting prints. To one side is a wonderful sheltered, secluded garden with chairs and tables on the lawn and marvellous views across the valley. Beyond the large car park is the Eskdale Cricket Club's spectacularly positioned ground; the pub is the club's headquarters, and also hosts the traditional Christmas meet of the local Hunt. Home-cooked food using local produce is available both in the bar and in the separate, intimate restaurant. The bedrooms are relatively simple but the breakfasts and the views make up for that. One word of warning, though: the pub has recently changed hands, so there may be changes in store.

King George IV

Tel: Eskdale (094 03) 262
On the valley road five miles east of Holmrook

✕ lunchtime and evening

Marston Pedigree; McEwan 70/; Theakston Best Bitter

The King George occupies a splendid position, right at the junction of the Eskdale road, which runs eastwards from the coast to Boot and the Hardknott Pass, and the sometimes narrow but certainly spectacular road over to Ulpha in Dunnerdale. (Take the latter road for two miles or so, to the point where the track to the remote tarn of Devoke Water leaves to the right, and you'll be rewarded with a sensational view across upper Eskdale to the Scafell range and Bow Fell). The miniature railway serves this pub too – Eskdale Green halt is only a hundred yards or so away. Until 1974 the pub was known as the King of Prussia, but following the outbreak of the

First World War it was considered prudent to change it! The only hostilities likely to break out now are those between customers jostling for position in the tiny bars, which are delightfully cosy and old-fashioned, and centred around a superb little bar counter. At the front of the pub there are a few rustic tables on a miniature patio, while there is a little lawn with some picnic tables round the back. The food at the King George is well known though the menu is a little predictable. There are also a few letting bedrooms at very reasonable prices; some have a grand outlook over the Esk to the slopes of Birker Fell.

GOSFORTH
Globe Hotel

Tel: Gosforth (094 05) 235
The Square

✕ lunchtime and evening

Theakston Best Bitter, XB

Gosforth, a residential village acting largely as a dormitory for the nearby Sellafield works, lies right on the boundary of the National Park and is best known as the gateway to Wasdale and as the home of a notable collection of Viking artefacts. The Gosforth Cross, in the churchyard of St. Mary's, is magnificently tall and slender; the base of the sandstone cross depicts Yggdrasil, the mythological ash tree on which the foundation of the Norse world was based. In the church are two "hogback" tombstones, intricately shaped and sculpted and representing contemporary Viking homes. The Globe cannot boast the same historical distinction, but is a warm and friendly haven, often busy and with a good reputation for its Theakston's ales. Painted brown and white, it stands at an angle to the main road through the village as it sweeps round a tight corner; the resulting triangular front patio has a couple of tables. The frontage is decorated with hanging baskets and pots of hydrangeas. The bar is simple, warm and friendly, with a roaring fire and scrubbed tables; children are welcome in a side room. The overall impression is one of a typically unpretentious west Cumberland village pub, but one which is wonderfully hospitable and eager to please.

RAVENGLASS
Ratty Arms

Tel: Ravenglass (065 77) 676
Half a mile from the A595, by Ravenglass station

✕ lunchtime and evening

Hartley XB; Jennings Bitter; Webster Yorkshire Bitter

Ravenglass is a remarkable place, magically situated at the combined estuary of the Esk, Irt and Mite, and with the remains of the Roman fort of Glannaventa, and more particularly its bath-house, Walls Castle, only a short walk away. It's a failed market town and decayed port – there was once a Saturday market and annual fair, and trade with Ireland was substantial until the seventeenth century. The more recent Muncaster Castle, with its defensive pele tower and famous gardens, can be approached by a splendid footpath from Walls Castle, or by road along the A595 past the restored Muncaster flour mill. As if all this were not enough, there is also the Ratty Arms, a highly unusual pub situated on the northbound platform of British Rail's Victorian railway station and close to the terminus of the Ravenglass and Eskdale miniature railway – La'al Ratty to its devotees. The Ratty Arms is an enterprising free house with a good line in food in the long, narrow bar, and, beyond a row of pillars and overlooking the main line railway, another narrow room with pine tables much used by families. For summer drinking there is a patio with some solid picnic tables overlooking the main Ravenglass car park and close to the interesting main street of the village – a street which peters out into the waters of the Esk at its southern end.

ST BEES
Manor House

Tel: Egremont (0946) 822425
Main Street (B5345)

✕ lunchtime and evening

if dining

Matthew Brown Bitter; Theakston Best Bitter

St. Bees is a fascinating and still quite big village perhaps best known now for its historical associations and the views of the town and its surroundings from the south; the beach is not all that popular. The settlement derives its name from St. Bega, who arrived from Ireland in the seventh century and founded a nunnery which developed into St. Bees Priory – destroyed by the Danes in the tenth century, rebuilt in the twelfth by the Benedictines and now represented only by St. Bees church. From the south the village is dominated by the high red sandstone cliffs around St. Bees Head – the most westerly point in Cumbria and the western terminus of the "coast to coast" walk. The Manor House is a former coaching inn on the long street which drops down into St Bees from the south; the pub lies facing the road at a slight bend towards the bottom of the hill, close to the railway station. A typical two-room northern town pub, it has a very cosy bar and a notably well-furnished and attractive lounge. Bar meals are on offer all day and are well worth a try; children's portions are available. There are also a few bedrooms, worth a thought in this comparatively quiet spot which is not all that far from the western dales.

STRANDS
Screes Hotel

Tel: Wasdale (094 06) 262
In the hamlet of Strands (Nether Wasdale) four miles east of the A55 at Gosforth

✕ lunchtime and evening

Theakston Best Bitter, Old Peculier; Yates Bitter

A pleasant country inn in a really beautiful setting, the Screes takes its name from the famous Wastwater Screes, a stony waste of jumbled rocks plunging down from the ridge of Whin Rigg and Illgill Head into the cold waters of England's deepest lake. And the screes are indeed in sight from the drive in front of the pub; the tables here, beneath the foliage on the front walls, and at the side of the pub have this splendid view. Food is available seven days a week and is taken very seriously, with large steaks and gammons something of a speciality; vegetarian and children's menus are available.

There is also a worthwhile choice of beer – most notably the excellent Yates bitter, dry and clean-tasting. A door at the right leads from the car park into the bar, which is quite narrow and – divided by archways – very long indeed, though on several different levels. At the far end is perhaps the most comfortable seating and also a family area; but the majority of the regular visitors don't get that far, preferring the conviviality of the little bar area immediately inside the door. The Wasdale fells are not far away, and there are superb walks at lower levels starting from the tiny little church in the hamlet.

Strands Hotel

Tel: Wasdale (094 06) 237
Opposite the Screes Hotel (above)

- ✕ lunchtime and evening
- **Hartley XB; Robinson Best Bitter**

A typical long, low whitewashed building standing directly opposite the Screes Hotel, the Strands is a traditional, small family-run hotel in the same marvellous location and equally close to the magnificent mountains at the head of Wastwater. There are a number of public rooms, including a spacious and comfortably furnished lounge bar with log fires in winter. Good, filling bar meals using local produce wherever possible are available here both at lunchtime and in the evening, with a chef's special changed on a daily basis. A small games room offers darts and dominoes. At the rear the very pleasant beer garden includes, to the great delight of families, a children's playground. There's plenty of local walking in and around Strands – also known as Nether Wasdale – including an excellent nature trail near the youth hostel at the lower end of Wastwater (expect to see plenty of rabbits at dusk!). Another attractive walk takes you over Irton Fell to lonely, uninhabited Miterdale and then to Eskdale Green, or try a longer expedition to Buckbarrow with a glorious prospect, from the crags on its southern slopes, of the high fells above Wasdale Head.

WASDALE HEAD
Wasdale Head Inn (Ritson's Bar)

Tel: Wasdale (094 06) 229
Eight miles east of the A595 at Gosforth. OS187089

✕ lunchtime and evening

Jennings Bitter; Theakston Best Bitter, Old Peculier; Yates Bitter

Tourism came late to Wasdale, and it was not until rock-climbers recognised the awesome possibilities of Scafell Crag that it began to be exploited. The first to realise its potential was the farmer and huntsman Will Ritson, who offered his services as a mountain guide and then astutely obtained a licence for part of the farm at Row Foot and renamed it the Huntsman Inn. As the reputation of the dale grew, "Auld Will" Ritson became celebrated as a great sportsman and true wit as well as "the world's greatest liar". The inn was rebuilt in the 1880s and its image improved by a further change of name, this time to the Wastwater Hotel. Since then it has become the Wasdale Head Inn, with an excellent, comfortable and recently renovated bar, Ritson's Bar (one of two memorials to the old man, the other being a small waterfall on the Mosedale Beck), which offers a very good range of real ale. There's also a decent selection of bar meals and, right at the entrance, an almost separate room with a roaring log fire which is

particularly useful for those with families or for walkers sodden from a day on the surrounding fells. Even better, in fine weather, are the tables outside by the beck, with a view upstream past the old packhorse bridge to Kirk Fell and Great Gable.

WHITEHAVEN
Central

Tel: Whitehaven (0946) 2796
Duke Street

✕ lunchtime and evening

Matthew Brown Mild; Theakston Best Bitter, XB, Old Peculier

The main entrance to this fine town-centre pub, strikingly painted in black and white, lies up a little outside staircase. Inside it has been very pleasantly modernised, with a few subdued prints and tasteful lighting making the comfortable lounge bar a particularly relaxing place to spend a few minutes away from the shops. The home-cooked food, very popular at lunchtimes, is interesting and appetising; the piped music tends to grate a little after a while, though. Closer acquaintance with the pub reveals a quieter back bar, much favoured by the locals (and the only bar with a handpump selling mild). This second bar tends to attract the older regulars in particular, and is a cosy, sometimes rather smoky, room with lots of mirrors on the walls. The Central lies on one of the streets forming the grid-iron pattern imposed by early town planners acting for the Lowther family during the town's rapid expansion in the eighteenth century to cope with the booming coal trade. Now the port is a good deal less busy, though the town has a number of interesting shops. Whitehaven was the venue for a rather bizarre American invasion, led by John Paul Jones, in 1778. Although he managed to sail his boat, the privateer "Ranger", into the harbour and set fire to a number of ships, it was not a resounding success.

Welsh Arms

Tel: Whitehaven (0946) 66288
Tangier Street

✕ lunchtime and Monday to Thursday evenings

Hartley XB

Even the brewery admit that "not so long ago the Welsh Arms was, to be perfectly honest, scruffy in the extreme". It has not been a Hartley's house for all that long, however, and considerable time and effort has been spent in transforming it into a really pleasant local, with new furnishings – admittedly a little heavy on the orange – and a few exposed black-painted beams. Plenty of prints around the walls also help to create a welcoming atmosphere. It's the first real ale watering-hole on the way into town from the bus and railway stations, and there's no better place to begin (or end) a drinking tour, itself a worthwhile proposition since Whitehaven can boast a number of fine pubs; we've chosen two but there are others such as the Anchor Vaults in the Market Place, popular with fishermen, and the excellent Sun Inn in Hensingham village which are well worth a try. Behind the Welsh Arms are remnants of Whitehaven's industrial past, and it's worth a stroll around the docks (part of the Old Quay is the original, dating from 1687) and along the Georgian streets in the town centre. Little is left of the former village of Whitehaven; even the church is part of the Lowther family's expansion scheme, with none of it older than 1693.

Although this is the smallest of the areas in this book it contains within it more diversity than most, and can boast some of the most famous sights in the Lake District – ranging from the splendid view of the Langdale Pikes towering above Great Langdale to the quaint little Bridge House in Ambleside. There are also the exceedingly popular Wordsworth shrines in Grasmere and Rydal – though there is much more to Grasmere than Dove Cottage – together with rapids and waterfalls at Skelwith Force, just below the marvellous little lake of Elterwater, and Colwith Force on the River Brathay west of Ambleside. In addition tourists could do much worse than to call in at the remains of the Roman fort at the head of Lake Windermere, and the showpiece village of Troutbeck, with its collection of late medieval "statesman" farmhouses.

Ambleside is a bustling tourist centre these days, yet the old heart of the village, in the area known as Above Stock, survives almost intact, only a stone's throw from *ye olde gifte shoppes* in the main street. The former church of St. Anne's, the old house of How Head, and the slate-grey farmhouses clustering around narrow streets make a worthwhile excursion, and the Golden Rule, a wonderfully unspoilt old pub, is close at hand on Smithy Brow. The pleasant, easy walk to High Sweden Bridge, a classic example of a Lake District packhorse bridge, starts from the old village. More crowded is the equally easy walk to the minor waterfall of Stockghyll Force, a favourite destination of the early tourists. Back in Ambleside itself, the tiny Bridge House, possibly built in the seventeenth century as a summerhouse for Ambleside Hall, is now a National Trust gift shop. Also worth seeing are the various mills, including a former cornmill which now houses a pottery; the low banks denoting the site of the Roman fort of Galava, right at the head of Lake Windermere; and Waterhead Bay on the lake, with the boat landing stages a hive of activity.

Grasmere is virtually synonymous with Wordsworth: the poet is buried in the churchyard and Dove Cottage, on the outskirts of the village at Town End, is the most visited of his homes. But there is also the church, the famous gingerbread shop, and the lake, lying some distance from the village but easily approached on foot. Grasmere

Clock: Golden Rule Ambleside

sports, probably the most famous of the district's many sporting events, attracts a huge crowd late in August. Rydal, just to the south, has the smallest and perhaps the prettiest of all the lakes, and also another Wordsworth house, Rydal Mount, where he lived for thirty-seven years. Dora's Field, behind the church, still sports a host of daffodils each Spring.

The Langdales, Great and Little, will be well known to most visitors. The Langdale Pikes dominate the views up-valley; the tourist route to their summits, via Stickle Tarn, is so heavily used that it has had to be extensively renewed. Beyond the Old Dungeon Ghyll, one of the best and most famous walkers' and climbers' hotels in the district, the scenery is more rugged, with the magnificent Bow Fell and Crinkle Crags at the dalehead. A narrow road connects the two Langdales, with Blea Tarn in an idyllic location between the two. Little Langdale has its own tarn, the photogenic Slater Bridge, once used by quarrymen heading for work on the flanks of Wetherlam, and the narrow, twisting road heading towards the Wrynose and Hardknott passes.

Troutbeck, separated from Ambleside by the notable viewpoint of Wansfell Pike, is a village which cries out to be visited, most particularly for Town End, a seventeenth-century farmhouse now maintained by the National Trust and crammed with fascinating artefacts (including an ancient mangle, a cheese press and a wooden washing machine). There are quite a few of these architecturally distinctive and picturesque farmhouses, originally the homes of "statesmen" or yeoman farmers, in the village, which consists of a number of hamlets connected by a maze of attractive lanes and tracks; in addition the church, in a hollow down by the Trout Beck itself, and the historic Queen's Head Inn are well worth seeing.

AMBLESIDE
Golden Rule

Tel: Ambleside (053 94) 2257
Smithy Brow

Hartley Mild, Fellrunners, XB

A gloriously unspoilt example of a traditional Lakeland inn, the Golden Rule has built up such a reputation that it is an obligatory stopping off point for many journeying through Ambleside. All this is despite its location, tucked away on the road to the Kirkstone Pass and therefore all but hidden from the main road through the town. There are three rooms, one of them often used by family parties, and all of them are hospitable; the main bar area is a haven of peace and quiet, ideal for a quiet conversation and regularly used for just that by walkers and climbers talking over the day's accomplishments or planning the next day's assault. The famous golden rule itself, a polished brass measuring rod, hangs behind the bar and originates from the infamous P1 fighter. Pub grub is limited to

Humping gas cylinders in nightie: Golden Rule

simple snacks and there are few frills, but the beer is seldom less than superb. As a result the pub is understandably highly popular with locals as well as tourists and can become quite crowded, but it exudes warmth and character and is an absolute must for the drinking tourist. Worth seeing nearby are the ancient farmhouse of How Head, partly constructed with stones from the Roman fort of Galava, the old chapel of St. Anne's, and the former corn, fulling and bobbin mills on the Stock Ghyll.

Ambleside: cheerful drinker with gloomy hare in the Golden Rule

Waterhead Hotel (Stringer's Bar)

Tel: Ambleside (053 94) 32566
Waterhead (half a mile south of the town centre on A591)

✕ lunchtime and evening

until eight pm

Jennings Bitter; Marston Pedigree

The Waterhead Hotel is a dignified grey-stone building overlooking the boat landings at the head of Lake Windermere; it offers three-star comfort in an exceptionally fine position and with easy access to most of the lakes and dales. The main part of the hotel was built in the eighteen-thirties by John Stringer – hence the name of the recently refurbished and now very comfortable lounge bar where the real ale is dispensed. Stringer's great achievement was to exploit the position of the hotel to ensure that the cocktail and lounge bars and the restaurant – and indeed most of the bedrooms – had superb views across Windermere to the low hills around Wray Castle. Stringer's Bar, perhaps at its most hospitable on winter nights when a roaring log fire creates a cosy atmosphere, offers guest beers in addition to the Jennings and Pedigree, a good variety of hot and cold dishes, and folk music on Friday nights. A really outstanding garden graces the front of the hotel, with elegant white tables and chairs on cropped grass which could pass for a putting green and which has an uninterrupted view of the lake. Waterhead is very busy indeed during the tourist season, with Sealink vessels calling at Ambleside Pier and a host of smaller craft available for hire or for guided tours of this most popular of lakes.

CHAPEL STILE
Wainwrights Inn

Tel: Langdale (096 67) 253
On B5343 at the west end of the village

✕ lunchtime and evening

Theakston Best Bitter, XB, Old Peculier

Though this is advertised as a "traditional Lakeland pub", it is in fact a recent conversion (and an impressive one at that) which has provided Chapel Stile, formerly a "dry" village, with its own pub. Wainwrights is part of the huge, and still growing, timeshare complex which has transformed much of the valley floor, formerly housing quarries and, surprising to many, a gunpowder works into an area of pine lodges with an exclusive club and up-market hotel. The pub, a big and imposing building in local stone, is of mock-traditional Lakeland style, with black beams and a partly stone-flagged floor. There is comfortable seating (apt to swallow up the unprepared!) around huge wooden tables. A wide range of bar meals is available, and these are certainly popular with tourists. Traditional pub games are featured, including a functional yard of ale. The inn enjoys a tremendous view across the narrow valley to the rugged, low fells opposite, including Silver Howe, and immediately behind the pub there is the wild, white water of the surprisingly wide Great Langdale Beck tumbling through rapids on its way to Elterwater. The narrow road from Chapel Stile across Red Bank to Grasmere has excellent views from several vantage points, though it is often congested in summer.

ELTERWATER
Britannia Inn

Tel: Langdale (096 67) 210
Off B5343 in the centre of the village. OS328048

lunchtime and evening

Hartley XB; Jennings Mild, Bitter; Marston Pedigree

There can be few more charming and peaceful spots than this to have a pint or two – or indeed to stay for a few days, for this excellent village local has a number of neatly furnished bedrooms and also a self-catering cottage. The Britannia, a white-washed stone-built pub, which is in fact an amalgamation of a group of seventeenth-century quarrymen's cottages, overlooks the village green in Elterwater. It is only a short walk past (of all things in this tiny village) a bowling green to the reedy shores of Elterwater – "swan lake" to the Norse settlers who named it. On a gravelly terrace in front of the pub are a few tables, and a couple more to the side, in a nicely laid-out garden. In busy periods the village green is itself pressed into service as an overflow drinking area, while Morris dancers sometimes perform there in summer. The cosy, old-fashioned bar to the right of the entrance has a slate fireplace and a relaxed atmosphere; a rather more basic bar at the back is much favoured by the locals. The food in the dining room is straightforward but nourishing and the dinners are very filling indeed. Until shortly after the Second World War the pub was called the Hare and Hounds; now the pub sign shows the ship of the line "Britannia", the sister ship of Nelson's "Victory".

GRASMERE
Tweedies

Tel: Grasmere (096 65) 300
At the rear of the Dale Lodge Hotel

- ✕ lunchtime and evening
- 🏵
- ☺
- **Theakston Best Bitter, XB, Old Peculier**

A lively pub where there always seems to be plenty going on, Tweedies is unusual in that it occupies the back end of a former hotel which now functions as a rest home for the retired. The pub's garden, which is large and very pleasant, is thus right next to the grounds of Dale Lodge, with relaxing drinkers and perambulating residents oddly juxtaposed. The garden, and even more the comfortable bar and family room, are havens of peace in this often overcrowded village. The pub offers friendly service, good food in the separate dining area, and well-kept beer.

The Britannia, Elterwater

It is a worthy successor to the Dove and Olive Branch (or, some would have it, the Olive-Bough and Dove), the former pub into which William and Dorothy Wordsworth moved in 1799, and which they renamed Dove Cottage. The Wordsworths' cottage is quite a stroll from Tweedies, but the centre of the village is nearer, with St. Oswald's church (the scene of an annual rushbearing ceremony on the Saturday nearest to St. Oswald's birthday, 5th August) and the poet's grave in the churchyard. Grasmere sports, the most important in the Lake District, are held on the Thursday after the third Monday in August (they really do work things out this way up here!), and they include Cumberland wrestling, hound trailing and the Guides Race, amongst the most famous of all the fell races.

LANGDALE
New Dungeon Ghyll

Tel: Langdale (096 67) 213
Off the B5343, five miles north west of Ambleside

✕ lunchtime and evening

Hartley XB; Matthew Brown Mild; Theakston XB, Old Peculier

The New Dungeon Ghyll Hotel is a solid stone building in a spectacular position beneath the Langdale Pikes and Pavey Ark. The well-worn path alongside Mill Gill (frequently but wrongly referred to as Stickle Ghyll) to Stickle Tarn and the Pikes starts outside its front door. The public bar is therefore very popular with walkers and tourists, some basking in a warm glow of satisfaction after having conquered Jack's Rake, the hair-raising scrambling route on Pavey Ark. Others may be found licking their wounds after finding that even the "stroll" to Stickle Tarn was rougher and steeper than they had supposed! The New Dungeon Ghyll was a farmhouse in medieval times (like its rival hotel, the Old Dungeon Ghyll, further up the valley) but has for many years been a comfortable hotel, the base for innumerable walking and climbing parties. The bar is surprisingly spartan, with tables derived from the bases of old sewing machines (still with working treadles) and various brands of snuff available over the bar counter. Occasional folk evenings are arranged when there is very much an "open house" policy, with allcomers encouraged to have a go. It's a friendly, outgoing sort of place – drinkers are warmed in winter by the real stove as well as real ale, and a good selection of bar meals is always available.

Old Dungeon Ghyll

Tel: Langdale (096 67) 272
Off B5343 six miles north west of Ambleside

✕ lunchtime and evening

Marston Pedigree; Theakston Best Bitter, XB, Old Peculier; Yates Bitter; Younger No. 3

Formerly a "statesman" farm on the sheltered south-facing slopes of Great Langdale, the Old Dungeon Ghyll is now a superbly situated hotel, boasting one of the most memorable settings in the Lake District. It has a quiet lounge bar reserved for residents, and a rather basic public bar with distinctly spartan furnishings but bags of character where a deposit has been known to be levied to reduce the impact of over-exuberant climbers on the stock of beer glasses. The hotel, affectionately known for generations as the ODG, has the added distinction of being the terminus for a useful bus service from Ambleside. The bar, with slate floors, an old black-leaded range and high-backed alcove seating, is old-fashioned but cheery, with maps and rock-climbing photographs on the walls; traditional pub games are provided, though sudden out-breaks of folksinging are just as popular. The oven over the fire comes into its own in winter as a favourite spot for drying socks and boots. There is a separate family area near the entrance, with a food bar. Excellent home-cooked meals are available in the bar or the dining room. The choice of beers is outstanding, and there are occasional guest beers to increase the range still further. All in all this is an experience not to be missed!

RYDAL
Glen Rothay Hotel (Badger Bar)

Tel: Ambleside (053 94) 32524
On A591

✕ lunchtime and evening

Hartley XB; Bass Special Bitter

The Glen Rothay, delightfully situated opposite Rydal Water, dates from the early seventeenth century and was originally number eleven of the Rydal "farmholds". In the nineteenth century it appeared in William Wordsworth's "Guide to the Lakes" in the guise of Ivy Cottage. Nowadays it is a welcoming country hotel with beamed ceilings, an oak-panelled residents' lounge and bedrooms, some of which look out over Dora's Field, immortalised by Wordsworth and now tended, daffodils and all, by the National Trust. Other bedrooms have four poster beds and one has a balcony overlooking the lake. The Badger Bar, with bench seating, bar stools and copper-topped tables, displays a variety of representations of animal life including stuffed foxes and owls in addition to the inevitable badger. It is renowned both for its Hartley's and its quite considerable collection of malt whiskies. A very substantial dinner is served at half past seven every evening in the dining room, and this five course affair has revived many a fellwalker; but the Badger Bar also offers bar meals for the smaller appetite. The large beer garden is a very popular destination in the tourist season.

TROUTBECK
Queen's Head

Tel: Ambleside (053 94) 2174
Town Head (on A592)

✕ lunchtime and evening

Webster Yorkshire Bitter; Wilson Original Bitter

The village of Troutbeck, consisting of several little hamlets clustered around ancient wells and with over a dozen "statesman" farmhouses dating from the days of the yeoman farmers in the seventeenth century, is an absolute must for the discerning tourist. In the most northerly cluster, Town Head, can be found the Queen's Head, a fascinating and historic country inn set in marvellous surroundings. An ancient hostelry with slate slab floors, it is best known for its Mayor's Parlour, which since 1779 has been the scene of the annual mayor-making ceremony. Admittedly the mayor these days is not desperately overworked: the sole duties are those of organising the annual hunt and naming his successor. Previously the mayor's main role was to mediate in any disputes which arose in the village. The Queen's Head now has, in addition to the Parlour, bars with the obligatory oak beams and an ancient fireplace. Perhaps the nicest spot though, especially on a fine evening, is by the tables outside the inn, with unsurpassed views across the valley of the Trout Beck (the course of High Street, the Roman road, runs unseen in the valley bottom here) to the Ill Bell ridge, with the Garburn Road, a packhorse track of considerable antiquity and importance, clearly seen descending the slopes of Yoke towards Troutbeck church.

A customer orders food

THE BUTTERMERE VALLEY AND COCKERMOUTH

There are three quite different lakes in this romantically scenic area, together with some magnificent mountains; and the pubs aren't bad too! Pride of place goes to Buttermere, a lake of great beauty – whether seen from near the little chapel in the hamlet of Buttermere, with the brooding mass of High Stile behind; from the lakeshore below Hassness, with the prow of Fleetwith Pike jutting forward at the top end of the lake; or end-on from the road leading up to the Honister Pass. The 'circular' walk around the lake is an exhilarating tour, whose highlights include the ravine of Sour Milk Gill, with water foaming angrily down the steep little valley after heavy rain, the view of the track leading up to the historic Scarth Gap Pass, the farmhouse at Gatesgarth and the buttercup meadows on the way back to Buttermere and its ancient inns.

Crummock Water, once joined to Buttermere but now separated from its sister lake by a flat alluvial plain, is a very different sort of lake. The scenery seems somehow harsher, with Rannerdale Knotts almost overhanging the lake on one side and the long wall of Mellbreak containing it to the west. Scale Force, dropping 50 m (170 ft) in a single fall and therefore the highest waterfall in the Lake District, is only half a mile or so from the lake shore (though quite a walk from Buttermere village), and from around here there are stunning views of Grasmoor End, its ascent an unrelentingly hard slog from the bracken-strewn common of Lanthwaite Green. The third lake is Loweswater, smaller but perhaps prettier than the other two, with an attractive wooded shoreline accessible from the road to Mockerkin – though the footpath through the woods on the opposite shore is an even better way to get to know the lake. The scattered village of Loweswater, centred on the excellent Kirkstile Inn, hosts a notable show and a vintage car rally each Autumn.

Further down the valley is Lorton, where the hall is reputedly haunted by a woman carrying a lighted candle, and Cockermouth, birthplace of William Wordsworth, with its ruined castle, the remains of the Roman fort of Derventio, and a colourful, busy market. Not far from Cockermouth is Eaglesfield, an attractive village in its own right (and one which has produced some famous sons) but also the home of the Black Cock, a delightful, unspoilt country inn. Cockermouth stands at the confluence of the Derwent and Cocker, and the enlarged River Derwent then runs down into Workington, not noted as a tourist destination but with an interesting history, having originated as a fishing village, been transformed in the nineteenth century into a port and coal mining and ironworking centre; now having to endure massive unemployment, with the mines closed and much of the docklands semi-derelict.

BUTTERMERE
Bridge

Tel: Buttermere (059 685) 252
On B5289

✕ lunchtime and evening

Theakston Best Bitter, Old Peculier

Buttermere village is of no great intrinsic interest but is beautifully positioned. The tiny nineteenth-century church in particular enjoys wonderful views over the lake to the tumbling waters of Sour Milk Gill and the High Stile range. The Bridge Hotel, in the village centre where the B5289 crosses the Sail Beck, was originally a corn mill but has been licensed since 1735 and has at various times been called the Bridge, the Queen, the Victoria and now the Bridge once more. It's a fine hotel in a tranquil spot, with a wide choice of walks around the lakes, to the notable waterfall of Scale Force, or on the high fells which hem the valley in on both sides. There are two bars – a very pleasant and well-furnished public bar with useful maps on the walls, and a light, spacious lounge bar with big chairs around low tables and patio doors leading outside. A separate restaurant is open in the evenings providing an imaginative menu and generous portions. Sample dishes include *poussin canoise*, *veal tyrolienne* and, to follow, fresh green figs in Pernod. At the rear, away from the main road but right opposite the Mountain Goat bus terminus, there is a really nice enclosed court-yard with plenty of tables and excellent views across the valley.

COCKERMOUTH
Brown Cow

Tel: Cockermouth (0900) 823174
Main Street

✕ lunchtime and evening

Theakston Best Bitter, XB, Old Peculier

Very well located, right in the centre of Cockermouth, the Brown Cow is an extremely popular pub at the junction of the Main Street and the road to Lorton and Buttermere. A short distance away is the attractive Georgian house which was William Wordsworth's birthplace. Nine windows wide and boasting a porch with Tuscan columns, it is one of the best houses in the town and (inevitably) is in the care of the National Trust, with a small exhibition in part of the house. While the Brown Cow cannot aspire to such distinction, it is a neat, compact little pub which has been thoroughly 'Theakstonised' by its former owners, Matthew Brown. The bars are pleasantly furnished and quite spacious – usefully so since they can become quite crowded at times. One of the features increasing the pub's trade is the interesting range of meals, in several different styles and encompassing a wide price range. A standard list of home-cooked meals is complemented by speciality steaks (including cowboy's specials), lots of burgers (chilliburger and venisonburger, to name but two), Mexican beef and beans, and pizza – this latter available to take away. A separate children's menu is also on offer. All in all, this pub is a sound choice for those marooned in Cockermouth.

Swan

Tel: Cockermouth (0900) 822425
Kirkgate

✕ lunchtime and evening

☺

⊞ **Jennings Mild, Bitter**

Kirkgate, which leads south out of Cockermouth's wide Market Place, is an agreeable urban street, all the more so because of the double row of trees along its length. The Swan, a neat cottage-style pub which makes its own contribution to the scene, is equally attractive inside and well worth the walk from the town centre. The cosy little low-ceilinged bar is full of character (and usually characters), decorated by a hop bine above the bar counter in the corner, and a variety of pictures on the wall, many with a canine theme. Through a low wide arch there is a small back bar and family room. The Jennings is impeccably kept, and a wide selection of single malts will tempt the whisky connoisseur. Bellringers from the nearby church came to this bar to be rewarded (in cash and in ale) for their services; now the local brass band uses it after practice. The Market Place (no longer used as such – there's a purpose-built sheep and cattle market now) has its origins in the grant of the town's first market charter in 1221. On the far side of this a lane leads down past the ruined walls of Cockermouth Castle to the buildings of Jennings Brewery, at the confluence of the Cocker and Derwent but actually obtaining its water from deep wells. The castle, dating from the twelfth century, occupies a glorious site and is sometimes open to the public.

EAGLESFIELD
Black Cock

Tel: Cockermouth (0900) 822989
Half a mile west of the A5086

Jennings Bitter

This one is an absolute classic: if you can't get to any other Jennings pub, make sure you visit the Black Cock. It's not that it serves amazing meals: you'll do well to find any food here. Neither does it have bars which attract customers as a result of their plush seating or elegant decorations. The Black Cock simply doesn't need that sort of attraction, and with luck it is not in line for change of any sort. It's simply a superb untouched alehouse, with simple chairs and bar stools (those for the locals have loose cushions), a few exposed beams and one wall wood-panelled. Above all, though, it has a timeless feeling and a superbly quiet, relaxing atmosphere. The pub is famous for its brasses – not just horse brasses but also brass candlesticks and even a brass bedpan. It may be somewhat off the beaten track (though within half a mile or so of the main road between Cockermouth and Egremont) but drinkers intent on a superb pint come from miles around. Outside there is no garden, but a tiny field where goats and chickens are often in evidence. The village, with a little green and a wide variety of house styles, has a number of famous sons, including Fletcher Christian, the well-known mutineer, John Dalton, founder of the atomic theory, and Robert Eaglesfield, founder of Queen's College, Oxford.

GREAT BROUGHTON
Broughton Craggs

Tel: Cockermouth (0900) 824400
Half a mile from A66, on the eastern edge of the village

✕ lunchtime and evening

Jennings Bitter; Theakston Best Bitter; Draught Bass

This spectacular country house hotel is a real treat for the beer drinker – especially the drinker who also likes to eat out! The Broughton Craggs, set in its own beautifully maintained gardens on the edge of Great Broughton, some three miles from Cockermouth, is well known for its very varied and well-presented food. There is a comprehensive à *la carte* menu, a recommended set menu and, for the somewhat less pecunious, a supper menu served in the handsome restaurant; almost everything is home-made. The traditional roast lunch on Sundays is exceptionally popular. The hotel, which began life as the 'manor house' and summer residence of a wealthy businessman in the early nineteenth century, and was opened as an hotel in 1976, has been refurbished to an extremely high standard, as witness the wide hall with its glistening chandelier and curving staircase. The accommodation (ten rooms in all) includes four-poster beds and a bridal suite. Non-residents are equally welcome in the elegant, sumptuously furnished lounge bar whose picture windows afford a marvellous view across the lawns and through mature trees to the Derwent valley and the grey outline of Brigham church, and the distant outline of the north-western fells beyond.

HARRINGTON
Ship

Tel: Harrington (0946) 830331
Harbour Side (near B5296)

✕ lunchtime and evening

Matthew Brown Bitter

Harrington, effectively two villages, High and Low, adjoins Workington and to a large extent is simply a residential extension of the old port and coal mining town. The remains of Dalzell's Brewery, which sold out to Matthew Brown in 1925, are incorporated in one of the village's garages. To reach the Ship, turn left off the main road, following signs for the marina and pass under the railway bridge. Once through the railway arch there is an amazing change of scenery, with a marina full of brightly coloured yachts to the right; a big grassy open space ahead and off to the left the beach. The Ship itself lies just on the left, a solid pink-painted building which actually looks much more impressive from seaward. It's wonderfully positioned next to the marina, which has developed out of the old harbour – originally constructed in 1670 – and is especially busy on marina day in July. It's also conveniently close to the beach, and a children's playground, and has its own outside drinking area. The food is surprisingly good, given the location of the pub and its rather stolid exterior; the house speciality is country crockpot cookery, which goes down well in the rather smart, well-proportioned lounge. There is also a very popular games room.

LORTON
Wheatsheaf

Tel: (090 085) 268
Low Lorton (B5289)

✕ lunchtime and evening (summer only)

Jennings Bitter

A straightforward village pub, not likely to be missed by those travelling between Cockermouth and Buttermere since it juts awkwardly out into the road, the Wheatsheaf is, like so many around here, long, low and white-painted. It is a comfortable, old-fashioned pub which is attractively arranged offering traditional pub games in the cosy public bar and a big lounge bar. The pub is full of character and repays an extended visit, not least for the consistently high quality of the Jennings bitter. The bar meals are worth a try too. At the back is a caravan site, with caravans to let – it's certainly well situated for touring the Buttermere valley, with fell walks over Red Pike and High Stile, and also up onto the Grasmoor plateau. Lorton is the original home of the Jennings brothers' venture into brewing, and part of their old malthouse now forms the village hall. Lorton Hall, which has the remains of a pele tower and other medieval fragments, hosted King Malcolm III of Scotland during one of his tours of the Kingdom of Strathclyde in the eleventh century, and in 1653 was visited by Charles II. It is reputedly haunted by a ghostly woman carrying a lighted candle.

LOWESWATER
Kirkstile

Tel: Lorton (090 085) 219
Seven miles south of Cockermouth, off B5289

✕ lunchtime and evening

Jennings Bitter

A magnificently situated old inn set in tranquil surroundings between two of the Lake District's least spoilt lakes, Loweswater and Crummock Water. Behind the trim little pub are the brooding slopes of Mellbreak, one of the lesser fells in terms of height but offering a pleasant climb, partly on rocky slopes close to Crummock Water. The hamlet of Loweswater comprises an ancient church, itself worth looking at, a few farmhouses and cottages, and the Kirkstile dating from the sixteenth century but tastefully renovated to provide a very pleasant setting. There is a cosy, beamed bar and a verandah lounge which benefits from excellent views of the low fell country around the hamlet. A garden slopes down to a beck running between tall oak trees, and for those with children, a barn has been converted into a family room, with jukebox and pool table. The very popular food is served for much of the day, and includes a separate children's menu (a further side room is available for family parties). There are ten bedrooms, three of them family rooms, in what is certainly a quiet place to stay. The peace is disturbed occasionally, however – the Loweswater Show is held here every September, and the Kirkstile is a popular hunting venue.

MOOTA
La'al Moota

Tel: Aspatria (0965) 20414
Immediately off the A595, four miles north of Cockermouth

✕ lunchtime and evening

☺

Wilson Original Mild, Original Bitter

Previous descriptions of this extraordinary, welcoming pub in such august publications as the *Good Beer Guide* make for interesting reading, if nothing else...'Landlord reputed to be the meanest in Cumbria', for example; or try 'Dominoes team is the worst in west Cumbria'; or 'Both regulars think it's great'. Not exactly the stuff which brewery advertising directors dream of, but then not many such people tend to visit the La'al Moota. That is undoubtedly a pity, for this amazing, friendly, cramped little pub might change their ideas a little. The heart of the pub is the front bar, two tiny rooms knocked into one, still tiny, room. There's hardly enough room for everything, let alone everyone who wants to squeeze into this vibrant hive of activity. Brass is very much in evidence, with a highly-polished pair of scales; there's an enormous wooden spoon and above the fireplace is a dartboard. In one corner is a creaking trophy cupboard (dominoes trophies?), in another is the tiny, curving bar counter. Outside at the front is a little lane, almost a private service road, below the main road from Cockermouth to Carlisle; at the back is a wonderful view over desolate moorland to the smooth slopes of the northern fells, with Skiddaw the focus of attention. Back inside, there's a tremendous welcome for regulars and visitors alike – as long as they don't mention dominoes, or indeed ask to see the benchmark.

WORKINGTON
Henry Curwen

Tel: Workington (0900) 67355
Bridge Street

✕ lunchtime

---

at lunchtime

Matthew Brown Mild, Bitter; Theakston XB

This is a smart town-centre pub, formerly functioning as the showpiece of the Workington Brewery. No longer: the brewery has been axed and there is a forlorn look about the massive, green-painted brewhouse tower across the way. Known by some as 'Galloping Harry's', the Henry Curwen is generally busy and certainly very efficient, with a reputation for high-quality bar lunches at a very fair price. It is a pub which has been fitted out in the grand style, with the single bar neatly divided by partitioning and subtle changes of level to give the feeling of several small rooms. A very long bar counter runs virtually the length of the room on the right, with plenty of standing space for the lunchtime crowds. At the far end, raised up a little, is a particularly nice drinking area with striking paintings around the walls. There's a library theme to much of the pub, with books and shelves dotted around, while the use of subdued lighting contributes to a pleasant, genial atmosphere. Plenty of dark wood, and the use of reds, browns and pinks for the decoration, emphasises this relaxed atmosphere. On the far side of the brewery the land drops away quickly to the Derwent valley and the home of Workington's soccer and rugby league clubs.

Miner's Arms

Tel: Workington (0900) 67216
Guard Street (by the roundabout at the junction of A596 and B5296)

✕ lunchtime

---

at lunchtime

Matthew Brown Mild; Theakston Best Bitter, XB

The last pub in Workington to be 'Theakston-ised' by Matthew Brown before they lost their independence, the Miners Arms is a small but very friendly corner pub on the eastern edge of the town centre. It is to be hoped that the change of ownership does not lead to a reversion to its former style, for the new Miners Arms has already built up quite a reputation for its beer and for the quality of its lunchtime bar food. Painted black and white in the usual Theakston style, it may not appear especially promising from outside, but once through the front door the warmth of the welcome in the two cosy bars is guaranteed to put visitors at ease. Traditional pub games are available in the bar, while the lounge has been neatly refurbished and is an ideal location for a quiet drink. As for Workington, it too promises little at first sight, but can claim Roman origins and had lords of the manor (the Curwen family commemorated in the name of the 'other' pub) who traced their ancestry back to Malcolm II of Scotland *and* Ethelred the Unready! The Curwens built Workington Hall in the fourteenth century; Mary Queen of Scots spent a night on the run there in 1568, after the Battle of Langside.

Keswick arouses mixed feelings, but this slate-grey town, a very popular destination on wet days, is never less than welcoming and boisterous. It has no great architectural or historic pretensions, but there's a good deal to do there now, and on fine days the sight of Latrigg and Skiddaw rising above the slate roofs is inspiring. Derwentwater, too, is only a short stroll from the town centre, with boating, walks along the lake shore and the noted Century Theatre. In the town there is the excellent museum in the tranquil setting of Fitz Park, with a scale model of the Lake District, manuscripts of the Lake poets, and some rather odd musical stones. There, too, is the Moot Hall, now housing an information centre; Greta Hall, the home for forty years of Robert Southey; interesting alleyways; and a number of rather good pubs.

Borrowdale will be familiar territory for many, who if nothing else will have driven along the eastern shore of Derwentwater, past Lodore Falls and the arched bridge at Grange, to the dalehead hamlets of Seatoller and Seathwaite – starting point for the walkers' routes over Sty Head to Wasdale, Great Langdale and, for those made of sterner stuff, to Great Gable and the Scafell Pikes – and then over Honister Pass to Buttermere. Particular attractions along the way are the Bowder Stone, a glacial erratic offering minor rock climbs, the side road to Ashness Bridge (the view across the lake to Skiddaw from here is one of the most photographed in the whole of the Lake District) and Watendlath, famous as the home of Judith Paris in Hugh Walpole's 'Rogue Herries' novels. The pleasant return journey is along the relatively uncrowded west side of the lake.

East of Borrowdale are the rather undistinguished mountains along the central axis of the high country, and then Thirlmere, which has belonged since 1879 to the Manchester Corporation Water Works and is still surrounded to a large extent by conifers, though access to the shores of the reservoir is much improved. Past the northern end of Thirlmere a road on the right off the main Keswick road leads through the very pleasant St John's in the Vale, passing under the Castle Rock of Triermain, important nowadays to rock-climbers but also the setting for Sir Walter Scott's 'The Bridal of Triermain'.

To the north of Keswick lies Skiddaw, a great mass of mountain country with several subsidiary summits as well as the ever-popular Skiddaw itself. Eastwards lies Blencathra, possibly the finest of the Lake District's major mountains, with a seemingly infinite variety of ways to the top: the best are perhaps Hall's Fell, which leads straight as an arrow to the summit from Threlkeld, and Sharp Edge, a knife-edge arete perched dramatically above the supposedly bottomless Scales Tarn. Looking northwards from either of these noble summits one can view Back o Skidda' country – mile after mile of rounded, green fells with no roads, few through footpaths and very few visitors. Skiddaw Forest, not a tree-covered forest but a hunting preserve, is nevertheless fascinating, as are the villages around the northern rim of the fell country. Of particular note are Caldbeck, home of John Peel, and with the substantial remains of former mills, one of them in the eerie limestone gorge known as The Howk; and two former market centres, Ireby and Hesket Newmarket.

BASSENTHWAITE
Castle Inn

Tel: Bassenthwaite Lake (059 681) 401
At the junction of A591 and B5291

✕ lunchtime and evening

🛏

Jennings Bitter

Traditional Lakeland hospitality is high on the agenda at this imposing three-star hotel close to the northern extremity of Bassenthwaite Lake. Originally a farmhouse, it is unrecognisable as such now; it developed first into a coaching inn for stagecoaches on the Carlisle to Keswick road, and then into a small hotel which has been progressively expanded over the last thirty years. The Castle (the derivation of its name is unclear) is noted for its *cuisine*, and the dining room offers superb views over the attractive and carefully maintained gardens of the hotel. The lounge bar, tastefully furnished and spacious, provides a very comfortable venue for a glass of Jennings beer or something to eat. The surprisingly ordinary saloon bar, with fruit machines and rather faded decoration, is doubtless due for refurbishment. Attractions in the near vicinity include sailing on Bassenthwaite Lake, fishing, and some of the best routes to the top of Skiddaw; further afield are the historic city of Carlisle, Wordsworth's birthplace in Cockermouth and John Peel's grave in the churchyard at Caldbeck.

Sun

Tel: Bassenthwaite Lake (059 681) 439
At the northern edge of the village, half a mile from the A591

✕ lunchtime and evening

Jennings Bitter

This is a well-established country inn in a compact village which, somewhat disappointingly, lies a couple of miles away from the lake of the same name. The heart of the place is the informal, irregularly-shaped green, surrounded by pleasant slate-grey houses, while the pub and a disused mill lie at the top of the village. On entering the pub through the elaborate porch one is confronted by a big, solid bar counter, but this somewhat daunting beginning is deceptive, for the atmosphere is pleasantly informal and the service excellent. The main lounge bar has plenty of nooks and crannies for a leisurely drink, while there is a quieter back room (where families are welcome) with a stone fireplace and comfortable bench seating. The special attraction of the house for diners is its wide range of Italian and Cumbrian dishes, with on the one hand *canneloni* and vegetarian *lasagne*, both served with garlic bread, and on the other game pie and Cumberland sausage. The mixture works well: the pub is unquestionably very popular for its food. Outside there are one or two tables, but not enough seems to be made of the opportunities for outside drinking in this attractive and quiet setting. Perhaps the experience of too many wet Lake District summers has had its effect!

BRAITHWAITE
Coledale Hotel

Tel: Braithwaite (059 682) 272
Above the village on the no through road into Coledale

- ✕ lunchtime and evening
- ❀
- ☺
- 🛏
- Younger XXPS (Scotch Bitter)

To find the Coledale Hotel, which is easily seen on its prominent site above the village centre but less easily approached by car, take the little lane signposted to the long, quiet valley of Coledale just after the road from Keswick to the Whinlatter Pass has threaded its narrow, twisting way through Braithwaite. This is a big, bustling place which has seen so much housing development in recent years that it now feels more like a suburb than a country village. The hotel stands apart from all this, in an imposing position and with a remarkable outlook over Bassenthwaite Lake to the rounded fells of the Skiddaw massif. Originally (in about 1820) the Coledale was a woollen mill; then the Cumberland Pencil Company was founded here in 1868, but it moved to its present factory in Keswick after a disastrous fire thirty years later. The Georgian country house which remained after the fire became a small hotel. There are two public rooms – the Georgian Bar, dating from 1824 and very pleasantly furnished, with many of the original features intact, and the 1899-vintage Victorian Lounge, which is reserved for diners at busy times. In front of the hotel, and quite sensibly making the best of the outstanding view of Skiddaw, is a grassed area with a number of picnic tables. Heavy emphasis is laid on catering, and there is a catholic range of main courses available, followed by desserts such as Granny Slinger's Parkin.

GOOSE GREEN
String of Horses

Tel: Raughton Head (069 96) 358

At the junction of B5299 and B5305

✕ lunchtime and evening

Marston Burton Bitter, Pedigree

In some ways this is one of the most difficult pubs to find, despite the fact that it lies at the junction of two B roads (from Wigton to Penrith, and from Carlisle to Caldbeck). But you will be lucky to find a sign to Goose Green, and there will be no one to help in this desolate, sparsely peopled area north east of the Caldbeck Fells. If all that sounds inhospitable, don't abandon the attempt to locate it, for once found in its totally isolated crossroads position the String of Horses will amply repay your efforts. It's a warm and cosy pub, with an especially nice little snug to the right of the entrance, quickly overcrowded sometimes by those in the know. To the left as you enter is a larger bar, quarry-tiled and spotlessly clean, but bright and cheerful too. At the far end there is a pool table and juke box; closer are the bar, selling a great pint of Pedigree, and a few plain tables around the fire. Though it no longer has strong horse racing connections the String of Horses is close enough to Carlisle racecourse to be convenient for celebrating successes or drowning sorrows as appropriate. It used to be a port of call for drovers of geese from Whitehaven to Carlisle – a somewhat implausibly indirect route, but then this friendly country pub does have its attractions!

HESKET NEWMARKET
Old Crown

Tel: Caldbeck (069 98) 288
On a minor road a mile south east of the B5299 at Caldbeck. OS341386

✕ lunchtime and evening

Hesket Newmarket Brewery Wrynose Light Bitter, Blencathra Bitter; Thwaites Best Mild, Bitter

A classic small village pub, tucked away in Back o Skidda' country close to Caldbeck. Already very well known for its excellent bar food, and especially its curries – the *rogan josh* has to be tasted to be believed – the Old Crown has recently branched out and now sports its own brewery. The home-brewed beers are certainly distinctive (Thwaites' beers are thoughtfully provided for those with conservative palates) but they add a welcome extra dimension of choice for pubgoers in north Cumbria. Of the two small bars, one is dominated by a pool table but the other bristles with character – and indeed with local characters. Black-painted beams adorn the ceiling, and around the walls are the volumes of a lending library whose proceeds (10p a book at present) help to provide guide dogs for the blind. There is a separate dining room for the curry fanciers and other *gourmets*. All this in a pub which acts as a focus for the very special village of Hesket Newmarket, a "green village" with an inordinately large central green dividing two rows of mainly limestone cottages and farmhouses, and an elaborate eighteenth-century market cross as a reminder that this was once a reasonably prosperous market centre, the scene of sheep and cattle fairs until the early nineteenth century.

IREBY
Sun

Tel: Low Ireby (096 57) 346
A mile south of the B5299.

✕ lunchtime and evening

Jennings Bitter

The Sun is one of two pubs in the quiet village of Ireby, tucked in a fold of the far northern fells west of Caldbeck. It's hard to believe that, like Hesket Newmarket, this was once a market town of some importance, with a Thursday market that was so successful that it threatened the future of Cockermouth, and an annual fair which flourished for over 400 years from its inception in 1237. The village is now much reduced in size, though it is by no means small even now, and the remains of the market place, Moot Hall and butter cross can still be seen. The Sun is a very good example of a traditional Cumbrian country inn, with two pleasant though far from plush bars. The bar to the right is perhaps the more attractive of the two, with a fine wood-burning stove, old-fashioned settles and pictures including a fascinating print of a horse and trap outside the pub in former days. Pub games available include darts and shove-ha'penny. Through a set of double doors is a peaceful, secluded garden with a few tables. The left-hand bar is perhaps slightly plusher and is certainly well patronised at weekends by the locals – though during the week I've been pretty well the only lunchtime customer in the pub. Food is served most of the time and ranges from nicely-presented sandwiches to substantial meals. It's a matter of regret that the beer is less well presented: the very weak keg beer, Lakeland Light, is dispensed here using a fake handpump. Fortunately the bitter is well worth drinking.

KESWICK
George

Tel: Keswick (076 87) 72076
St Johns Street

✕ lunchtime and evening

Theakston Best Bitter; Yates Bitter

The George, an old and rather pleasantly old-fashioned coaching inn only a few strides from the Moot Hall in the middle of Keswick, is one of the great compensations for wet days in the northern fells. That eagerly anticipated walk or climb may have to be abandoned for the day, but a pint in the George is a rare luxury too. Originally the George and Dragon, this, the oldest inn in Keswick, adopted its shortened name upon the accession of George I. There's a tremendous sense of history in the air, for this was the place where the German miners came with their silver and lead from Newlands in the sixteenth century to pay their dues to the revenue officers. It was here too that the Earl of Derwentwater stopped for his last drink in Keswick before joining the 1715 rebellion and

Family snug
The George,
Keswick

subsequently losing his head at the Tower of London. And here, after the place had been remodelled in Georgian times and adopted a new identity as a coaching inn, was where Wordsworth, Coleridge and Shelley came to drink. The snug on the left (now used by families at lunchtimes) and the front parlour bar on the right have changed little since their time. The bar, right at the back of the inn and approached across an attractive quarry-tiled floor, between posts and pillars, dispenses excellent real ale, and the food, in the bar or the restaurant, is never less than filling. A nineteenth-century brochure claimed that the George "positively invites the weary traveller to step inside for rest and refreshment and to finish the day's journey there with a substantial meal and good bed". Not too much has changed at this excellent old inn.

Pack Horse

Tel: Keswick (076 87) 72536
Pack Horse Court, Main Street

- ✕ lunchtime
-
-
- **Jennings Mild, Bitter**

This is a very welcoming, totally unpretentious pub in one of the several alleys – variously known as yards or courts – which run down from Keswick's Main Street and market place towards the River Greta. In one of them, King's Head Yard, there is the former home of the clockmaker turned celebrated geologist Jonathon Otley. Pack Horse Court is perhaps more altered than many of these narrow alleys, with their little stone-built cottages now largely turned into shops and offices, but whereas Woolpack Yard and King's Head Yard, amongst others, have lost their pub, the Pack Horse continues, with a choice of rooms including comfortably lived-in bars and a more modern lounge (not always open). There is also a patio in Pack Horse Court itself, facing a row of shops including one selling excellent prints of local scenes. In common with most Keswick pubs, the Pack Horse can get extremely crowded on summer nights. It is worth postponing the sightseeing stroll around Keswick – a worthwhile excursion with the nineteenth-century Moot Hall, neat red sandstone parish church with a fine view of Derwentwater from the churchyard, and art gallery and museum in Fitz Park – in order to claim a table and then sit back and soak in the atmosphere at this very pleasant pub.

Pheasant

Tel: Keswick (076 87) 72219
Crosthwaite Road

- lunchtime and evening
- **Jennings Bitter**

Until the fourteenth century Keswick was little more than the dairy farm which its placename implies. The mother church of Keswick and the whole of Borrowdale was St Kentigern's at Great Crosthwaite, and this church, reputedly first built in 533 AD but rebuilt in the twelfth, fourteenth and sixteenth centuries, still repays a visit today. No longer, however, do people "come in a great concourse to Crosthwaite Church every Sunday to buy and sell corn, flour, beans, peas, linen and

cloth, fish and flesh"! Quite close by, on the Carlisle road (A591) out of Keswick, is the Pheasant Inn, one of the best pubs in Jennings' tied estate and a firm favourite with many. The meals served in the dining room from a distinctly adventurous menu have a high reputation, and the draught bitter is pretty good too. The bar is cosy and welcoming, with panelling and an open fire, and the decoration is enhanced by a bevy of cartoons featuring larger than life characters. Many of them depict hunting scenes, understandably so since this is the venue of the annual Boxing Day Hunt. There is also a patio for warmer days, and the accommodation, though limited, is good quality. The brewery certainly likes this pub: it was featured in a recent television commercial.

Twa Dogs

Tel: Keswick (076 87) 72599
Penrith Road

✕ lunchtime and evening

Jennings Mild, Bitter

This modern pub, which takes its name from the famous Rabbie Burns poem 'A Tale of Twa Dogs' (go on! you must have heard of it) is hugely enjoyable, not least because it offers the chance to see the only known *bogart vulgaris* ever captured. Not surprisingly, the pub is the headquarters of the Cumbrian Bogart Preservation Society. The stuffed and mounted bogart, a rather fearsome-looking cross between a fox and a badger, occupies pride of place above the fireplace, and there are photographs around the bar of its spectacular attempts to evade capture. It may also be worth warning potential customers of the pub that the landlord of the Twa Dogs has in the past made off with the title of biggest liar in the world... Darts and pool are on offer in the bar, which is a big room with spacious alcoves, but egg dumping and the duckathlon are taken equally seriously. There's a good choice of food available at the bar, and the beer is good too – compelling reasons for visiting this amiable if slightly crazy pub which is handily situated near the start (or end) of the recently-developed Railway Walk to Threlkeld and sufficiently away from the overcrowded centre of Keswick. The accommodation is equally highly spoken of, clean, comfortable and very reasonably priced.

PORTINSCALE
Farmers Arms

Tel: Keswick (076 87) 73442
At the western edge of the village, near the Keswick by-pass
OS248237

Jennings Mild, Bitter

A small and quite basic locals' pub on the edge of Portinscale, included primarily as an alternative to the sometimes bustling, overfull, tourist-oriented pubs of nearby Keswick. Long and narrow, its shape dictated by its position at the junction of converging roads and tracks, the Farmers has a single bar with a handful of formica-topped tables and one or two rather intimidating notices (especially the slate slab proclaiming "Ted's Corner" at one end of the bar counter: who else would dare to sit down there now?). To a large extent the pub *does* cater for local drinkers – their personal beer mugs compete for hooks above the counter – but tourists are quickly put at ease too. It is primarily a no-frills drinkers' pub, though certainly none the worse for that. There's dartboard, juke box and, in a small room at a lower level, a fruit machine and pool table. Photographs on the walls testify to the more outrageous catches of local fishermen. The food is restricted to snacks but the beer is worth the journey – perhaps from Keswick across the suspension footbridge over the River Derwent, a replacement for the Long Bridge which was gradually weakened and then finally swept away in the floods of 1955. Nearby Lingholm Gardens, famed for rhododendrons and azaleas and therefore at their best in June, are well worth a visit, and Portinscale also acts as the gateway to the beautiful and still relatively unspoilt Newlands valley.

ROSTHWAITE
Scafell Hotel

Tel: Borrowdale (059 684) 208
On B5289

- ✕ lunchtime and evening
- river terrace
- **Theakston Best Bitter, XB, Old Peculier**

Rosthwaite, with its inns and village shop, is the focus of life in upper Borrowdale and is also an excellent base for walking: there are some very pleasant bed and breakfast places away from the main road, too. It has not always been as quiet and respectable as it is now, however, for Nooka House, once an inn and after that the post office and sweet shop, was well known for card playing and dancing, the former at least of somewhat dubious legality. The origins of the Scafell Hotel can be traced back to the increase

Billy, 36yrs
at Riverside Bar
Scafell Hotel

in tourism in the nineteenth century, which prompted the conversion of a substantial private house into a coaching inn relying on travellers journeying over the Honister Pass on their scenic route from Keswick to Cockermouth. Its erstwhile owner, a Miss Barker, had once played hostess to the Wordsworths – the poet stayed the night in Rosthwaite in 1812, sharing a bed with a Scotch pedlar, but reputedly did not seem to mind. Real ale is available in the Riverside Bar of the hotel, a plain public bar of no great distinction but leading on to a very nice riverside terrace overlooking the fast-flowing Stonethwaite Beck just before it joins the River Derwent. Rosthwaite, which stands on a little rocky spur above the flood plain of the Derwent, is in the centre of attractive walking country, with excellent excursions to Castle Crag and also over Grange Fell to Watendlath. William Gilpin made this latter journey in 1772, describing the climb up from Rosthwaite as lying "up a lofty mountain steeper than the tiling of a house". A slight exaggeration, perhaps... following a visit to one of the Rosthwaite inns?

SCALES
White Horse

Tel: Threlkeld (059 653) 241
On a miniature by-pass off the A66

✕ lunchtime and evening

Jennings Bitter

This is a friendly, popular roadside pub at the foot of Blencathra and very close to the point where the well-trodden path to Scales Tarn, Sharp Edge and eventually Blencathra's summit leaves the fast, busy A66. It lies on the old Keswick to Penrith road at a point where a bend has been straightened out and a very short stretch has been declared redundant except as an impromptu car park for the pub. The White Horse is an unassuming, low, whitewashed building with its windows picked out in black. From the bar windows on this side there is a view right across the Glenderamackin valley to the northern outliers of the Helvellyn range, with the old Matterdale coach road visible on the flanks of Clough Head. Once inside, the pub gives an immediate impression of warmth – perhaps not unconnected with the fireplace at either end of the long, narrow low-ceilinged lounge bar – and

White Horse Inn, Scales. Hunting mad...

an especially informal atmosphere. It is said that some of the low beams were originally ship's timbers, and certainly their unusual shapes support that theory. The walls are decorated with a variety of artefacts, some reflecting the proximity of the Blencathra foxhounds. The bar food is well-presented and reasonably priced.

SWINSIDE
Swinside Inn

Tel: Braithwaite (059 682) 253
On a minor road from Portinscale to Newlands. OS243217

- ✕ lunchtime and evening
- ❀
- ☺
- ⛟
- ⊕ **Jennings Bitter**

This is a really tremendous country pub, surprisingly popular with tourists given that it's a little way off the beaten track, but also drawing on a loyal local clientele. From the bar itself, and especially from the tables on a little terrace and in the garden there are stupendous views across the valley of the Newlands Beck to the unmistakeable knobbly summit of Causey Pike. A number of the bedrooms have this view, too, and this together with the exceptional welcome, the Jennings beer and the splendid breakfasts make

Stuffed otter: White Horse Inn, Scales.

the Swinside a very fine place to stay. One of the best all-day walks in the area, the Newlands Round, has the Swinside tantalisingly in sight but well out of reach for much of the journey! The bar, low-beamed and dating from the seventeeth century, is long and narrow but is neatly divided into a number of comparatively self-contained areas with comfortable bench seating and little bar stools. Considerable emphasis is put on the bar meals, which are as substantial as the breakfasts. It's a place where the buzz of conversation is never absent, much of it emanating from behind the bar. The games room has a pool table, but most of the activity takes place around the bar counter; it's worth the detour from the main road to sample it!

THRELKELD
Horse and Farrier

Tel: Threlkeld (059 683) 688
A quarter of a mile from the A66

✕ lunchtime

☺

Jennings Bitter

Threlkeld, an interesting mixture of old farmhouses and cottages, nineteenth-century mineworkers' terraces and more recent speculative development, is now bypassed by the A66 and is therefore both quiet and shielded from overdevelopment for tourism. One popular tourist attraction, though, is the annual sheepdog trials, held on the third Wednesday in August. The Horse and Farrier blends perfectly into the village, an uncompromising sort of pub which has a certain amount of tourist trade but also caters for mountain rescue teams, fell-runners, hunt followers, and rugby devotees. The view of the pub from across the road is exceptional: the long low white building, with its superb pub sign, is dwarfed by Blencathra, its ridges and deeply-riven gullies rising steeply behind the village. Above the door is the inscription "C I G 1688", commemorating Christopher and Grace Irton, the then owners of Threlkeld Hall and also of the newly-built pub. Notable visitors in the past were De Quincey and Wordsworth who stopped here for afternoon tea every Tuesday after Wordsworth had swallowed his pride, asked Lord Lonsdale for a job, and become Distributor of Stamps for Westmorland. Inside the pub there is a side room with pool table, where families are also welcome, and a big main bar, old-fashioned but all the better for that, with a notable fireplace, somewhat spartan seating, local notices and a dominoes corner where the game is played very seriously indeed.

Jack Coulston,
ex-lead miner, The White Horse, Scales

Salutation

Tel: Threlkeld (059 683) 614
A quarter of a mile from the A66

✕ lunchtime and evening

Matthew Brown Mild, Bitter; Theakston Old Peculier

This is a pub which grows on you – indeed, the pub itself almost appears to grow as more and more rooms and other facilities are discovered. At first it seems to be a simple one-room village local, with a bar area where most of the locals congregate and, neatly partitioned from this, a more comfortable though rather cramped area much favoured by tourists to whom the food – which is excellent – is perhaps as important as the beer. Closer inspection reveals a third area through an archway, with quarry-tiled floor, low tables and hatch service from the bar. And intimate knowledge reveals, through a doorway and upstairs, perhaps the best family room in the Lakes, big and very well appointed, with a pool table. And at the back of the pub, fronting onto a narrow lane, is a little patio area with lots of summer flowers and a few tables. A few hundred yards to the east are the remains of the Woodend and, a little higher up the valley, Gategill lead mines, responsible for a Klondike-style rush of activity towards the end of the nineteenth century, when Threlkeld was transformed from a sleepy agricultural village into a busy mining village. Now just the spoil heaps and derelict buildings remain, though at Gategill (where the Blencathra foxhounds are kennelled) a path leads quickly up onto Hall's Fell and the slopes of Blencathra itself.

ULDALE
Snooty Fox

Tel: Low Ireby (096 57) 479
Two miles from B5299. OS250369

✕ lunchtime and evening

Tetley Mild, Bitter

Uldale, a peaceful and quite scattered agricultural village, lies secluded in the Ellen valley, deep in Back o Skidda' country, but that doesn't prevent large numbers of people from converging on this imaginatively modernized village inn. The Snooty Fox image is everywhere, though – there are even top-hatted red foxes on the deep blue carpet! The main lounge bar is light, airy and spacious, with a blue and white theme and plenty of pine; it is a big room but cleverly designed so as to appear less so, with a number of distinct drinking areas. Families are welcome here, and plenty of them seem to come, for it's a very popular eating spot not far from the northern tip of Bassenthwaite Lake. The standard of bar food is very high, and the service is efficient, assured and friendly. In front of the pub are some picnic tables on a rather formal patio – mind the step, though, in entering the pub from here! In Hugh Walpole's Rogue Herries novels David's home was set in Uldale, and Judith Paris escaped through a window here prior to her journey on horseback across the fells to Squire Gauntry's house in the nearby village of Caldbeck. Further up the Ellen valley is Over Water, an almost unknown tarn, and then, beyond Orthwaite, the green road which leads past the Whitewater Dash waterfalls to Skiddaw House, a former shepherd's hut in an astonishingly remote location.

WYTHOP
Pheasant

Tel: Bassenthwaite Lake (059 681) 234
Just off the A66 as it skirts the north end of Bassenthwaite Lake. OS199307

- ✕ lunchtime and evening
- ❀
- ☺
- 🛏
- ⊕ **Draught Bass; Theakston Best Bitter**

A splendid long, low, whitewashed country inn dating back some 400 years and now standing somewhat away from the much-improved A66, though still quite close to the lake and near the sailing club. Behind the Pheasant are the northern outliers of Thornthwaite Forest cloaking the flanks of Sale Fell. Even the porch is impressive, with flowers in big tubs beneath vegetation which curls up and over the porch itself. There's an aura of old world warmth and hospitality inside, in wonderfully traditional, cosy bars which have roaring log fires, antique but beautifully preserved furniture and lots of nice touches including fresh flowers in strategic places. In the bar itself, neatly divided into two rooms, there are oak settles and ochre walls and ceilings from centuries of tobacco smoke. The bar food, much of it home-made, is very good and certainly very filling. Most people elect to eat in the restaurant, though meals are also available in the large lounge bar, with its view over the very pleasant garden behind the inn, which slopes down to the beech woodlands and is in a notably peaceful setting. The bedrooms at the Pheasant, homely and neat, are very popular in the season – and indeed for winter weekends too. A short drive south along the A66 there is a quite magnificient view across Bassenthwaite Lake to Skiddaw, one of the four English mountains (all in the Lake District) which reach the 3000 feet mark.

The River Eden, though it is the unifying feature for much of this area on the eastern fringe of the Lake District, will only be glimpsed by those who travel to sample the pubs in Appleby (and to take a look around that most historic of towns). Otherwise only the western tributaries of the river are in view, notably the Eamont, which drains Ullswater and runs from Pooley Bridge, where the Sun Hotel is a venerable hostelry, to Eamont Bridge south of Penrith; the Lowther, which joins the Eamont there and the Lyvennet, which runs close to the unspoilt village of Morland.

But it is Ullswater which fires the imagination: a glorious lake of three distinct stretches, with outstanding scenery all the way, from the craggy mountains (including Helvellyn) crowding in around Glenridding and Patterdale to the gentler Dunmallet Hill above Pooley Bridge. There are so many treasures: Place Fell and the walk beneath its rocky slopes from Glenridding to Howtown (with the return journey by boat to Glenridding Pier); the splendid Aira Force, one of the best (and most accessible) waterfalls in the Lakes; the low hills to the east of Pooley Bridge, with prehistoric stone circles and a Roman road on Moor Divock, a great place for walkers with its wide views into the Lake District and also away to the Pennines in the east; and the village of Dacre with its historic church and a castle built around a medieval pele tower.

The market town of Penrith is worth a prolonged visit, not just for the three contrasting pubs included here but also for a tour of its red sandstone castle, a frequent target of Scots border raiders in their heyday, its church with startlingly thick walls and its collection of big, irregularly-shaped market places, including the site of the old cattle market in Great Dockray. Appleby, on the other hand, has its famous horse fair to boast about, together with its castle and a station on the historic but threatened Settle to Carlisle railway line.

Families touring in this area will inevitably make for Lowther country park, where there is a variety of attractions including boating, a model railway, go-karts, monster slides, an assault course and a circus. The beer there is nothing to write home about, however, so it's worth holding on until one of the excellent pubs nearby can be visited – perhaps the unspoilt George & Dragon at Clifton or the welcoming Queen's Head at Askham. Askham, an Anglian green village, became an estate village for Lowther Castle, whose frontage (and not much else) stands forlornly in parkland near the river. Further up the Lowther valley is the Helton Inn, highly recommended, and the road to Haweswater, the undeniably ugly reservoir whose creation led to the drowning of the village of Mardale Green – the somewhat eerie remains of which, including the renowned Dun Bull Inn, can still be seen during times of drought.

Woman smashing the lads at dominoes

APPLEBY-IN-WESTMORLAND

Royal Oak

Tel: Appleby (0930) 51463
Bongate

✕ lunchtime and evening

Yates Bitter; Younger Scotch Bitter

Appleby, probably most famous now for its annual horse fair, was the county town of Westmorland until 1974, and much earlier was annexed by Scotland for a while – until eventually William Rufus won it back for England in the late eleventh century. The Royal Oak lies in the oldest part of this historic town – indeed the area around Bongate was known as Old Appleby in medieval times. It is a delightful old black-and-white coaching inn dating from the seventeenth century (with parts believed to be several centuries older than that), with leaded dormer windows, wooden porch and colourful hanging baskets. The inn lies close to the River Eden, with Appleby Castle also close at hand. The cosy, wood-panelled taproom, highly valued by the locals, is an absolute gem, while there is also a pleasant little snug and a lounge bar which, with its old oak beams and real fire in winter, supplements the Yates' ale with a wide selection of malt whiskies. The dining room, open to non-residents, has a beamed ceiling and a notable collection of antiques, and is the perfect spot to round off a day on the eastern fells or in the Eden valley. Although there are only seven bedrooms, the facilities are excellent and all the ingredients for a relaxing break are provided.

Tufton Arms Hotel

Tel: Appleby (0930) 51593
Market Square

✕ lunchtime and evening

Marston Burton Bitter, Pedigree

The Tufton Arms is a solid, rather old-fashioned but very pleasant hotel right in the middle of Appleby, with the parish church of St Lawrence only a few steps away to the left, the market place with its little stalls in front, and the Moot Hall, on its island site and still used as a council chamber, immediately to the right. Further right is the grand old street of Boroughgate, fringed by lime trees and climbing the hill to the castle. Appleby Castle, with wonderful views of the countryside of the Eden valley from the high Norman keep, was the home of the Clifford family for seven centuries and is now home to a conservation centre approved by the Rare Breeds Survival Trust, with waterfowl, owls, pheasants, finches and parrakeets, some of them extremely rare. Appleby also has a station on the scenic but threatened Settle to Carlisle railway line, and in June hosts the famous horse fair. The Tufton is a superb base for all this, but is also useful as a venue for a quiet lunchtime drink and a bar meal from the quite elaborate menu. The lounge bar to the left of the entrance is used by locals as a convenient town-centre rendezvous, and certainly fulfils that function admirably.

ASKHAM
Queen's Head

Tel: Hackthorpe (093 12) 225
Off B5320 four miles south of Penrith

✕ lunchtime and evening

Vaux Samson (occasionally); Ward Sheffield Draught Bitter

Both village and pub are a real find. The Queen's Head stands in the centre of the village, its neat white-painted exterior beckoning the visitor. Over the gabled porch there is a stylised portrait of Queen Elizabeth I, while on the wall are a pair of wagon wheels salvaged by a previous landlord when the old Bampton hearse was declared redundant. But the most attractive feature is the magnificent array of flowers outside the front of the pub in summer. Inside there is a lounge bar to the right of the big entrance hall, with a curving bar counter and comfortable seating around the walls, and beams and brasses in abundance. Another, rather more intimate, lounge is situated behind the cross-passage. There is also a dining room in the former stables, converted now that the packhorse trains no longer call here. The meals, and in particular the steak suppers, are popular locally. In the garden a working model railway attracts children and adults alike. The village forms part of the Earl of Lonsdale's extensive Lowther estate, and indeed the ruined shell of Lowther Castle is just down the road. A little further is the adventure park which is fast becoming the most popular attraction in the Lowther domain. Askham village itself is a good example of an Anglian green village, with farmhouses and cottages set around a long, narrow central green on either side of the Haweswater road.

BAMPTON
St Patrick's Well

Tel: Shap (093 16) 224
Three miles north west of A6 at Shap

- ✕ lunchtime and evening
- ❀
- ☺
- Marston Burton Bitter

The highly unusual name of the pub recalls the legend of the Irish saint, St Patrick, who is reputed to have walked (preaching the while, of course) to Bampton after having been shipwrecked on Duddon Sands in 540 AD. The pub is rather too ordinary to fit well with this sort of distinction, but it is the nearest decent watering-hole to Haweswater and the excellent fells at Mardale Head. Try the superb ridge walk up Long Stile to the top of High Street (the course of a Roman road can still be seen on top of this mountain), or take an easier stroll to either of the

passes, Gatescarth or Nan Bield. The St Patrick's Well will look even more promising on your return – a little cottage pub with a tiny patio in front and a big bar, quite comfortably furnished, to the left of the entrance passage. The Marston's is a bonus in such an out-of-the-way place, and there is an appetising range of bar meals on offer. For those less inclined to struggle up mountains the local sights include Bampton Grange, originally an outlying grange farm of Shap Abbey, and down in the valley of the Lowther, the abbey itself, whose massive tower was completed only just before the Dissolution and forms the major survival.

BLENCOW
Clickham Inn

Tel: Greystoke (085 33) 406
On B5288 three miles west of Penrith

✕ available lunchtime and evening

❀

☺

⊞ **Marston Burton Bitter, Merrie Monk, Pedigree**

Totally unpretentious but nevertheless very welcoming, the Clickham Inn is an attractive roadside pub which will surely suit most tastes. Standing isolated from any settlement, and a long way to the south of Blencow village, it is of necessity a sturdy, four-square symmetrical building of local stone – a typically north country construction. It's very comfortable inside, with a huge variety of customers – from the convivial groups enjoying animated conversations at the bar to the more intimate (or shy) in little window alcoves or tables by the fire. It is a popular spot for Penrith office workers to head for when in need of a quiet drink in the country or an excellent bar meal. The service is friendly and super-efficient and the Marston's is seldom less than superb, too. Along the road towards Penrith is the Greystoke Pillar, sadly *not* the Pillar of a Wordsworth sonnet (that distinction belongs to the Countess' Pillar two miles the other side of Penrith). Dacre Castle, with its gaunt pele tower, Dalemain – a country house with a much more lived-in look to it – and the northern reaches of Ullswater, including the National Trust's Gowbarrow Park, are other local attractions.

CLIFTON
George and Dragon

Tel: Penrith (0768) 65831
On A6 at south end of village

✕ lunchtime only

Tetley Bitter

This excellent example of a traditional Cumbrian inn is set at an angle to, and quite a long way back from, the busy main road between Penrith and Kendal. It forms the middle part of a row of cottages, with only its porch and a big multi-coloured sign depicting the eponymous St George and dragon setting it apart from the private houses on either side. The bar oozes character which it has managed to retain despite recent renovation, and it is to be hoped that the increasingly rare phenomenon of waiter service, a notable feature here for so long, survives the changes. There are a few tables in front of the pub, around the fringes of a car park which is bordered on three sides by a magnificent display of flowers, and to the south by a very well-kept vegetable plot. Clifton itself is a straggling village of no enormous merit – with the exception of Clifton Hall, a late fifteenth-century battlemented pele tower which bears eloquent testimony to the turbulent times of Scottish border raids in the later medieval period and which is very well seen on entering the village from the north. The George and Dragon is nonetheless a popular stopping off point for those heading for or returning from Penrith and the eastern fells.

EAMONT BRIDGE
Beehive

Tel: Penrith (0768) 62081
On A6

✕ lunchtime and evening

Hartley XB; Whitbread Castle Eden Ale

This is a typically welcoming though quite unassuming roadside inn, with a very strong local following – there are quiz leagues, darts and dominoes teams and the bar is popular with the farming community – but with a very warm welcome for visitors too. The pub, dating from the early eighteenth century, is situated fairly close to Lowther Country Park, with its circus, boats, trains, assault courses and the like, and is therefore very popular with families; the garden includes a fairly well-equipped play area with swings, seesaw and a slide. A separate children's menu is offered too, to accompany a reasonably adventurous selection of assorted grills, curries and other delicacies. A recommended dessert is hot chocolate fudge cake. Above the front door the pub sign waxes eloquent:

In this hive we are all alive
Good liquor makes us funny
If you be dry step in and try
The virtue of our honey.

Virtually opposite the Beehive are the confusing mounds and hollows of King Arthur's Round Table, a circular double-entrance henge monument, while the much more impressive Mayburgh henge, its encircling bank still reaching a height of fifteen feet, is only a few hundred yards up the road to Pooley Bridge.

GLENRIDDING
Glenridding Hotel (Ratchers Tavern)

Tel: (085 32) 228
On A592 at the southern end of Ullswater

✕ lunchtime and evening

Tetley's Bitter

Glenridding is beautifully situated near the head of Ullswater, with the delectable Place Fell on the opposite shore of the lake and the lower slopes of the Helvellyn range crowding in from the west. There are boat trips along Ullswater from Glenridding Pier, calling at Howtown and Pooley Bridge, and delightful spots such as Grisedale and Angle Tarn, the latter with its magnificent mountain views, are easily visited. In the middle of all this is the Glenridding Hotel, large and imposing and well situated with lawns running down towards the lake. The lake tends to dominate the choice of activities, with sailing, windsurfing and (with care) swimming all available nearby, but there is also pony trekking on the lower fells. After all this a glass of real ale in the Ratchers Tavern may be considered particularly well-earned, and there will be those who graduate to the hotel's restaurant, with its nightly special dishes and vegetarian menu. The Ratchers itself does food, however, albeit somewhat more informally, with light lunches and bar suppers. It is a pleasantly relaxed sort of bar, big but well broken up and comfortably furnished.

There is live music on some evenings during the summer, but the warm, friendly welcome is available every evening.

HELTON
Helton Inn

Tel: Hackthorpe (093 12) 232
In the hamlet of Helton, six miles south of Penrith

- lunchtime and evening
-
-
- self-catering
- **Theakston Best Bitter, XB (summer)**

Beautifully situated on the road to Haweswater, the Helton Inn is notable for its garden: a few rustic tables on a patio immediately outside the pub and then, down a few steep steps, a lawn with more seats and plenty of space for children to run around while their elders enjoy the Theakston's ales, the excellent home cooking and the wonderfully wide view to the east, across the wooded, walled Lowther wildlife park. This is a favourite spot for those en route for, or more likely returning from, Haweswater and the fells around Mardale Head, but another lesser known yet very attractive walking area is even nearer. This is Moor Divock, a fascinating little part of the Lake District reached by taking the narrow lane in Helton, past the picturesque

farm at Heltonhead and out into open country. Park where the Pooley Bridge track goes off to the right and follow this green lane through the bracken, past the Cop Stone and mysterious cairn circles to the line of a Roman road (High Street) and a prehistoric stone circle (The Cockpit). There are exceptional views over Ullswater to the Helvellyn range from here. Then back to the Helton Inn, this time perhaps for a drink in the traditionally furnished, plain but very homely bar, with friendly and efficient service assured and plenty of convivial company as the evening wears on.

MORLAND
King's Arms

Tel: Morland (093 14) 328
Water Street

✕ lunchtime and evening

Marston Burton Bitter, Pedigree

A notable, unspoilt village pub which is outwardly perfectly ordinary but is really warm and cosy inside. It's tucked away at the bottom of a hillside village with a church whose Saxon tower is unique in Westmorland and Cumberland, and with attractive views over the Eden valley. Opposite the pub is the reed-fringed course of a little river, a tributary of the Lyvennet, and parallel to this a mill leat, controlled by a simple sluice gate a little further upstream. It's worth strolling a couple of hundred yards upstream to see, from a white-painted footbridge, the rocky weir and sluice gate, the latter crossed by a single-slab bridge, on one side and the old ford on the other. It's almost a picture-postcard scene, and since Morland is by no means on any tourist itineraries it's one you'll have to yourself, or at worst have to share with a few ducks and the village children. Back at the pub, an end-of-terrace cottage painted in two reasonably restrained shades of pink and adorned with hanging baskets, there'll be an excellent pint waiting for you together with a straightforward range of basket meals and snacks. The two rooms are small and relatively plainly furnished, but there is a very friendly atmosphere, with roaring fires in winter and the crackle of country conversation.

PENRITH
Agricultural Hotel

Tel: Penrith (0768) 62622
Castlegate

✕ lunchtime and evening

Marston Burton Bitter, Pedigree, Owd Rodger

One of the best town pubs in Cumbria, the Agricultural is full of character and, to the great credit of the brewery, this has been retained and even enhanced in recent renovations. The most notable feature architecturally is the elegant, intricate Victorian bar, a superb example of its kind. For many of the customers the chief distinction, perhaps, was the pub's extended opening hours on market days (Monday, Tuesday and Thursday); it stayed open until five o'clock, allowing horse-trading and banter in equal measure after the rigours of the market. Naturally the pub's very popular with the farming

Lovely woodwork in the Agricultural

community, not least because there's direct access from the bar to the auction mart next door. Flexible licensing hours may dilute that tradition, but the wonderful atmosphere of the old pub will remain, the conversation aided by the excellent Marston's ales and the good, wholesome and inexpensive food on offer. There's a welcome absence of distractions, too, with the landlord opposed to fruit machines and juke boxes. There's also an outside drinking area, and those who become really addicted to the place can stay overnight, in simple but comfortably furnished rooms. Literally round the corner, for those who can tear themselves away, is the

gaunt sandstone ruin of Penrith Castle, a favourite target of the marauding Scots during the days of the border raids.

Museum Inn

Tel: Penrith (0768) 63576
Castlegate

✕ lunchtime and evening

Hartley XB; Jennings Mild, Bitter

The Museum has built up quite a reputation under a succession of landlords, with the present incumbents maintaining the tradition of the place as a relaxed, informal watering hole just outside the town centre towards the castle and railway station. Unprepossessing from the outside, this 200-year-old inn has a splendid single bar, plain and homely, but very lively and full of local characters. Serious beer drinkers come to

Grandfather clock - the Agricultural, Penrith

sample the excellent ales (an odd but very welcome selection in what is in fact a Whitbread tied house); others are more concerned with the tasty food on offer (at lunchtime and until eight o'clock in the evening); while still others are simply there for the local gossip. If you're staying overnight the chances are that closing time or later will find you ensconced on a bar stool thoroughly enjoying the crack. Families are welcome in the small, cosy side room, which fulfils a different purpose in the evening as the meeting place for a wide selection of local societies, ranging from the jazz club to the local mountaineering group. There is occasional live music (not just from the jazzmen!), but generally the only sounds to be heard are the low rumble of traffic on Castlegate outside, the gentle buzz of conversation, and the pulling of yet another pint of real ale.

Woolpack

Tel: Penrith (0768) 63919
Burrowgate

✕ lunchtime

☺

Vaux Samson

Burrowgate is one of several irregularly-shaped open spaces in the centre of Penrith which used to form specialised market places. Sandgate was the home of the weekly stock market (and the unsavoury sport of bull-baiting), Great Dockray saw the cattle fairs, Corn Market's function was self-evident, while Burrowgate saw trade in a variety of goods including woollens and fresh produce. Now the street, though right in the middle of Penrith, is tucked away behind the George Hotel near the clock tower, and the Woolpack too is easily missed by those taking the A6 straight through the old sandstone town. It's very much worth finding, though, since it is one of the few remaining traditional drinkers' pubs in the centre of Penrith, a warm and friendly, essentially one-roomed pub of enormous character. Though there are snacks available these are clearly secondary to the

Samson, over which a good deal of loving care is lavished – to good effect. In summer a wonderful display of window boxes brightens the exterior of the little pub, and it comes as no surprise to discover that it is a regular entrant in the "Vaux in bloom" competition. For a view on a wider scale, over the Lake District fells and the Solway plain, it's worth journeying from the pub to Penrith Beacon, once part of England's communications system and now a well-known viewpoint.

Woolpack, Penrith

POOLEY BRIDGE
Sun Hotel

Tel: Pooley Bridge (085 36) 205
On B5320

✕ lunchtime and evening

Marston Burton Bitter, Pedigree

An old coaching inn close to the northern end of Ullswater. Records relating to the Sun date back to the sixteenth century, and even the newest parts of the building are one hundred and fifty years old. It is comfortably the oldest surviving building in a village which was once an important market centre (as witness the widening of the main street where the markets and fairs used to be held) but which has declined in importance since the nineteenth century, when fish markets and a September sheep and cattle fair were still held. Now the village survives mostly as a tourist centre, and certainly the Sun is often very busy during the season, when the ferry service along Ullswater, calling at Howtown and Glenridding Pier, draws in the visitors. There are also some pleasant drives in the vicinity, notably along the eastern shore of the lake to Martindale, and westwards to Dacre, with its pele tower and interesting church; and good walking, especially on Moor Divock where some prehistoric stone circles and the remains of a Roman road can be seen. The inn, right in the centre of the village, has a very good reputation for food, with lunch and dinner available in the restaurant and a wide variety of bar snacks in the nicely furnished and comfortable lounge.

TIRRIL
Queen's Head

Tel: Penrith (0768) 63219
On B5320

✕ lunchtime and evening

Matthew Brown Mild, Bitter

A typical Lakeland country inn on the road from Penrith to Pooley Bridge and Ullswater, the Queen's Head was once a pair of cottages, one with the date 1719 above the door. It has developed quite a bit since the days of its first conversion, and is now a low-ceilinged inn with original beams, big stone fireplaces, and collections of brasses and pewter. The Queen's Head has quite a reputation for its bar food, which is generously proportioned; the speciality of the house is pies, all, they boast, individually home-made "to the highest quality of old-fashioned country baking". There's steak and kidney, of course, but also turkey, ham and chestnut; Victorian pie; and duckling and pigeon pie. The sweets sound mouth-watering, too, with blackcurrant *bavarois* among them. Children are welcome in a well-furnished lounge to one side of the main bar, and they have their own menu. The pub used to sell a pretty distinctive beer as well, from Tirril's own brewery, Siddle's. Admittedly memories of those days are a little dim – the village brewery closed in 1907. There are a couple of tables outside at the front, though these are right next to the road, which can be quite busy at times. Ten letting bedrooms are available for those needing a bed for the night conveniently close to the eastern lakes and fells.

YANWATH
Gate Inn

Tel: Penrith (0768) 62386
Off B5320 a mile west of Eamont Bridge

✕ lunchtime and evening

Theakston Best Bitter; Younger No. 3

A little cottage-style pub close to the main line railway to Scotland, the Gate Inn has an attractive bar, low-ceilinged and black-beamed in true Lake District style, with a roaring fire and bucket seats fashioned from barrels. Towards the back of the pub the bar becomes a restaurant (quite a shock in a pub of this size) where excellent and filling meals are served. It is very much a family pub, with a family room to one side and also an excellent beer garden, through an archway to the side of the pub, with big umbrellas protecting drinkers from the scorching Lakeland sun. At the front of the pub a gate swings high above the door, inscribed with the legend, quite common with pubs of this name:

This gate hangs well
And hinders none
Refresh and pay
And travel on.

The frontage is particularly nice, with hanging baskets and pots of flowers, and the date 1683 above a window. Beyond the railway can be seen Yanwath Hall, worth a look for its very fine example of a defensive pele tower, dating from 1323. The sandstone battlements stand out above a massive tunnel-vaulted ground floor, and next to it are the hall, kitchen and courtyard, added in the fifteenth century.

Carlisle is probably best known, in the context of visits to the Lake District, as a destination somewhat reluctantly chosen by those forced off the northern fells by the weather. But there's a great deal more to it than that, with a Norman castle, cathedral, excellent museum and lively city centre to explore. This border city has changed hands on numerous occasions, and is the only place where both the Scots and English Parliaments have met. The castle, dominant rather than picturesque, had to withstand repeated Scots raids in medieval times, and has a twelfth century keep within thick curtain walls. The red sandstone Carlisle cathedral, of considerable historical interest, has been the cathedral church of Cumbria for over eight centuries. The museum, in the Jacobean Tullie House, has impressive collections relating to local prehistory, Roman archaeology (with a number of exhibits from Hadrian's Wall), natural history, toys, dolls, and musical instruments. And the city centre, with modern stores in The Lanes and a pedestrianised area in English Street, is also worth seeing.

Although the line of Hadrian's Wall lay through Carlisle, there is little to be seen in the immediate vicinity; but it's not far to Birdoswald, off the A69 before Greenhead, where the five-acre site of Camboglanna Roman fort stands on a ridge overlooking the Irthing gorge. Substantial parts of the walls and gateways have survived, together with parts of the original turf wall. A little to the west of this lies Lanercost Priory, founded in 1166 and with its nave still intact and in use; also nearby is Naworth Castle, home of the Earls of Carlisle for the last seven centuries and with notable tapestries in the Great Hall. South of Lanercost and Naworth is a more modern attraction, Talkin Tarn country park, with sailing and boating, windsurfing, canoeing, fishing and, right on the spot, a really outstanding country pub.

West of Carlisle there are no such licensed gems, but the area around Bowness-on-Solway is fascinating. The village overlies the westernmost fort on Hadrian's Wall, while just to the east is Port Carlisle, at the seaward end of the Earl of Lonsdale's Carlisle canal. The canal was completed in 1823 but was a financial disaster and was replaced by a railway (also now gone) in 1854. The lock chambers giving access to the sea can still be traced. To the south of the city is the Eden valley – notably picturesque at Wetheral – with distant views of the Pennines, including the romantically named King's Forest of Geltsdale, and of the northern outliers of the Lake District. Also in the remarkably flat and quite sparsely populated area south of Carlisle is the racecourse, with National Hunt racing throughout the winter, and a remarkable Romanesque church at Wreay.

BROADFIELD
Crown

Tel: Southwaite (069 93) 467
Six miles south of Carlisle.
OS408464

- ✕ lunchtime and evening
- ❀
- ☺
- ⊕ **Matthew Brown Mild, Bitter; Theakston XB; regular guest beers**

This is an outstanding pub set in splendid isolation at a crossroads some six miles south of Carlisle, and three miles south of Carlisle racecourse. The A6 is only three miles away, near Wreay, but narrow lanes and a couple of junctions have to be negotiated from that direction. It's a very popular venue before and after racing, with the "Sporting Life" much in evidence and a plethora of hot tips (many of them bitterly regretted within hours) available before the event. The sporting theme is carried through in the pub's decoration, with the walls supporting quite a number of hunting scenes. There is only one bar but it certainly feels like three: a central area with the cramped bar counter groaning under the weight of four handpumps, a "public" area with games to the left, and a cosy room to the right where the locals tend to gather and where the rattle of dominoes can often be heard. Families are very welcome – indeed, *everyone* is made welcome: it's an astonishingly friendly pub. Many will be tempted by the promise of varied bar meals, available at pretty well all times; others come for the beer, which includes a good selection of guest real ales – Harviestoun Own Ale from Dollar in Clackmannanshire the latest to be spotted.

CARLISLE
Coach and Horses

Tel: Carlisle (0228) 32529
Kingstown Road (A7), 600 yards south of M6 junction 44

- ✕ lunchtime and evening
- ❀
- ☺ if dining
- ⊕ **Matthew Brown Bitter; Theakston Best Bitter, XB**

The Coach and Horses is an excellent roadside inn on the main road south into the city. It is very close to the new Asda superstore, and there must be quite a few drinkers who have adjourned here after a particularly gruelling session pushing a trolley. The design and layout is typical of the State Management Scheme, but sadly the revered SMS beers are no longer on sale across the bar. There is a relatively small, plain but well-furnished public bar, and an extensive lounge bar which has ancient-looking but clearly not all that old timber beams. The bar meals are excellent and attract customers from a much wider area than just the Carlisle suburb of Kingstown. Another notable attraction, this time on Thursdays only, is the regular quiz night, which is open to allcomers (and very nearly compulsory, so seriously is it taken!). There's a garden, too, which is well used in better weather. Within striking distance of the pub are surviving sections of Hadrian's Wall (whose course lay nearby, through the northern suburbs of the city, but can no longer be traced there), the excellent country park at Talkin Tarn, and the quieter border countryside around Longtown and Liddesdale.

Friars Tavern

Tel: Carlisle (0228) 23757
Devonshire Street

✕ lunchtime

Hartley XB; Whitbread Castle Eden Ale; Whitbread guest beers

This is a lively, easy-going city-centre bar close to Carlisle station and the "Citadel" – the Assize Courts, built in 1811 on the site of, and following the layout of, Henry VIII's citadel with its two round towers and courtyard in between. The Friars cannot boast such architectural distinction, and indeed its entrance is further disfigured by the grotesque life-size friar on an advertising hoarding, allegedly tempting passers-by inside. For those who are tempted, however, the delightfully informal atmosphere of the place soon takes over. To a large extent the convivial nature of the Friars is due to the welcoming friendliness of the hosts; it's said that the landlord has a particular interest in the study of distillery ceilings (ask about it if you dare!). Real ale – including a draught beer from the Whitbread selection, such as Wethered's SPA – is available in the downstairs bar, in many ways a typical city centre lounge bar which seems almost out of place in Cumbria. It is long and narrow but nicely compartmentalised, and has "stained" glass windows to the front. There is a well-regarded restaurant in the upstairs bar at lunchtime (it's available for private functions in the evening). Legend has it that an underground passage once connected the Friars to the cathedral – a not unlikely tale given the pub's name.

Howard Arms

Tel: Carlisle (0228) 32926
Lowther Street

✕ lunchtime

Matthew Brown Mild; Theakston Best Bitter, XB, Old Peculier

Visually pleasing both outside and from within, the Howard Arms is a very busy city-centre boozer, and deservedly so. How the superb, highly unusual tiled frontage has survived in a city centre street is a mystery, but the fine green and white brewery advertising is mercifully intact. Inside there are four small, cosy rooms served from a central bar, all attractively furnished and enlivened with theatrical memorabilia from the former Carlisle Theatre, which was located just across Lowther Street. Even these four rooms often prove insufficient at weekends, when the clientele is apt to overflow into the compact but beautifully-kept garden (the landlord's pride and joy!) at the back of the pub, and even into the street at the front. The bar lunches are another notable feature, not only excellent in themselves but representing very good value for money. The Howard Arms was the first pub in the area to be "Theakstonised" by Matthew Brown, and the XB in particular is a treat to drink. One of the entrances to the new shopping centre, The Lanes, is within a matter of yards, so the thought of a pint must tempt hundreds of reluctant shoppers every day. It's a pub where the customers, who are themselves very varied in age and style, seem to count for a great deal – to such an extent that there is even music in the toilets!

Woolpack

Tel: Carlisle (0228) 32459
Milbourne Street

lunchtime and evening

lunchtime and until eight pm

Jennings Mild, Bitter

Well within walking distance of the castle, cathedral and city centre, the Woolpack is a large local revered by real ale drinkers for the consistently high quality of the beer it serves (so good that Scamp, the resident dog, won't touch keg or cider), and perhaps just as much for the extraordinary welcome accorded by Jim and Moira to all and sundry. After a short time in the pub you'll feel you've been a regular for years! The pub is quite close to the ill-fated Old Brewery in Caldewgate (successively run by the State Management Scheme, Theakston and Matthew Brown and finally axed a year or two back). Following modernisation some ten years ago the Woolpack now has a large, comfortable L-shaped lounge with a remarkable wood-panelled ceiling, a snug little bar area and a games room complete with the inevitable pool table. Dominoes is perhaps the game played most fanatically here, however. A notable feature is the superb mural depicting the history of Carlisle. An interesting range of high quality bar meals makes a welcome change from the standardised fare available (still) in too many of Cumbria's pubs. A final word of warning to those tempted to stay too long: Scamp is renowned for his kangaroo impersonations at closing time....

GRETNA
Solway Lodge

Tel: Gretna (0461) 32866
Annan Road

lunchtime and evening

Broughton Greenmantle Ale; Jennings Bitter; regular guest beers

True, even the most elastic definition of the Lake District doesn't usually stretch quite as far as Scotland; but this terrific hotel is *right* on the border, in a busy tourist centre just a few miles north of Carlisle, and sells a relatively new Scottish real ale which perhaps ought to be better known. Essentially, though, it's simply too good to leave out. There's a nice, unpretentious but perfectly comfortable lounge bar (undergoing renovations in 1988) which is, under Scotland's liberal licensing laws, open all day every day – yes, including Sunday – and a splendid restaurant. The Solway Lodge has a fine reputation for its food, which is really good value, and the accommodation offered is also very pleasant. The key to it all is the very friendly and helpful reception which customers will receive, whether it's a bed, a meal or just a pint which they need. As for Gretna, a neat little town which is slowly shedding its one-track reputation as a quick hitching-post for English elopers, it is also a useful jumping-off place for the quiet Border hills around Newcastleton, for Kielder reservoir and for the fascinating towns of Hawick and Jedburgh. Closer to home the road to Annan and Caerlaverock Castle, along the Scottish side of the Solway Firth, makes for an interesting trip.

HAYTON
Stone Inn

Tel: Carlisle (0228) 70498
Half a mile south of A69

lunchtime and early evening

Hartley Bitter; Jennings Mild; Tennents 80/-; Theakston Best Bitter

A gem! The Stone Inn is a small L-shaped one-roomed village local with an especially convivial atmosphere. It was the first pub south of the border to sell Tennents 80/ , and it's nice to see that the landlord keeps faith with this ale, which is sadly rare in "real" form. The choice of beers offered is indeed catholic, if not downright idiosyncratic, but this is a conscious policy which is carried through to the spirits, offered in quarter-gill measures (big enough to Scots drinkers, simply massive to the unprepared English) and including excellent rum. No bar meals are served as such, but there is a wide and interesting range of *toasties*, including haggis. It is hard to believe that this tranquil village pub is only a few miles from the outskirts of Carlisle and within a very short distance of the busy trunk road to Newcastle. This is indeed a wonderful place to come and unwind, though not over a quiet drink, for the landlord will be at pains to ensure that all his customers can take part in and enjoy the "crack" at the bar. Traditional pub games including darts and dominoes are available, but the important thing is simply being there. It's a sad fact of modern life that there aren't enough pubs like this one left; make sure you give it a try!

LANERCOST
New Bridge Hotel (Blacksmiths Bar)

Tel: Brampton (069 77) 2224
A mile north of the A69 at Lanercost Bridge. OS553633

✕ lunchtime and evening

Ruddles Best Bitter

This is a pleasantly situated hotel by the beautiful medieval bridge with its two elliptical arches over the River Irthing, between Lanercost Priory and Naworth Castle. Real ale is available in the Blacksmith's Bar, which dates from the seventeenth century and was in previous times a forge, now superbly converted to provide a comfortable drinking area including a cosy, galleried dining area above the lounge bar itself. Meals are available at lunchtime and until nine in the evenings, and are well-regarded locally. The hotel was one of the victims of the noted temperance leader, Rosalind, Countess of Carlisle, in the late nineteenth century, but thankfully it has emerged from its "dry" phase to provide a decent pint once more. Lanercost Priory, an Augustinian foundation dating from 1166 and troubled frequently thereafter by Scots raids, is only a few minutes walk away and is well worth seeing, with ruined choir and transepts but a nave which is still very much in use. Naworth Castle, home of the Earl and Countess of Carlisle, is open in summer; the Great Hall has tapestries and is guarded by heraldic beasts. Less culturally satisfying but more fun, perhaps, is Talkin Tarn country park, offering windsurfing and sailing within a few minutes' drive of the New Bridge Hotel.

LOW HESKET
Rose and Crown

Tel: Southwaite (069 93) 346
On A6

✕ lunchtime and every evening except Monday

Marston Burton Bitter, Pedigree, Merrie Monk (occasionally)

An excellent village inn at the side of the A6, here on the line of the Roman road between Luguvalium (Carlisle) and Voreda (Old Penrith). Between Low and High Hesket is the Court Thorn, where tenants of the two villages previously assembled to pay their feudal dues. The Rose and Crown once sold the excellent State Management Scheme beers, and the pub itself is a superb example of a latterday flight of decorative fancy on the part of the Scheme. There is a light, airy but at the same time quite comfortable bar with the dartboard taking pride of place above the fireplace and plain seating around the walls. The lounge is cosy and attractively arranged, and there is also a family room. The place is well known for its excellent bar food, which is fairly straightforward but wholesome and very good value. The Marston's is never less than good, and on rare occasions the strongest mild in the country, Merrie Monk, can be sampled. At the front of the pub there are a few tables on a paved area below the A6 but protected from it by low railings; it has to be said, though, that this is not the most restful of places for a drink! What makes the pub special, perhaps, is the guarantee of a genuinely warm welcome, both from the landlord and from the notably friendly natives.

TALKIN
Hare and Hounds

Tel: Brampton (069 77) 3456
Off B6413
Closed Mon–Fri lunchtime, except July and August

✗ lunchtime (July and August, plus weekends) and evening

Hartley XB; Theakston Best Bitter, XB, Old Peculier

The only pub in the book where an order for a pint of XB is likely to confuse, this is an award-winning country inn of the very highest quality, with excellent real ale, food and accommodation. It's close to Talkin Tarn, a lovely spot but one which now, as perhaps befits a country park, gets very crowded in summer. Legend has it that the tarn is the site of a submerged town, but the long list of available activities, from boating to fishing, sailing and windsurfing is likely to prove more important to younger members of the family. The Hare and Hounds is closed at lunchtimes as shown above; evening opening is normal (though it may be seven o'clock before the pub opens). The new licensing laws may, of course, change all this in 1989! Once a resting place for monks on their way from Armathwaite to Lanercost Priory, the pub is unexceptional from outside, cottagey in style and has park benches beneath the windows. Inside, though, the style of the pub is very traditional, with old beams, antiques, very attractive stone fireplaces and a superb bar with fine etched glass. The meals are out of this world and there is a special children's menu at very reasonable prices; it's good policy to reserve a table if you plan to eat here during the evening. A house speciality is baked potato meals.

WETHERAL
Crown

Tel: Carlisle (0228) 61888
On B6263

✗ lunchtime and evening

Thwaites Bitter

Wetheral is an attractive village, delightfully situated on the banks of the River Eden, and now functioning largely as a residential dormitory suburb of nearby Carlisle. The Crown, a Grade II listed building next to the river and also very handily situated for the reopened railway station (on the Carlisle to Newcastle line) has in the last few years been very extensively altered and enlarged, and is now an imposing up-market hotel with squash courts, swimming pool, conference facilities, function room and thirty new bedrooms. Specialising in fishing holidays, it is Thwaites' most northerly tied house and in addition to being prized as the purveyor of an unusual real ale for the area it also has an excellent restaurant, the Conservatory, overlooking floodlit gardens, offering French and English *cuisine* and local specialities. The hotel, its frontage seven bays wide and sporting a classical porch with Ionic columns, stands close to Wetheral's village green. The lounge bar is very comfortable, indeed plush, reflecting the Crown's long tradition of hospitality. Big, soft settees, high-backed chairs, polished tables and pleasant prints, and a good deal of greenery all combine to create a relaxing but refined atmosphere.

Killoran Hotel

Tel: Carlisle (0228) 60200
On B6263

- lunchtime and evening
- **Ind Coope Burton Ale; Jennings Bitter**

Another hotel in this pleasant village and, in Burton Ale, another unusual beer for Cumbria. It's a very different kind of hotel, though, smaller and with perhaps a greater emphasis on (and opportunity for) friendly and personal attention. A comfortably furnished former mansion house opposite the village green, it is very popular for its good range of well-presented bar meals. An excellent garden offers lovely views over the River Eden and a decent children's playground – a nice and much appreciated touch. The Killoran's lounge bar, cosy and welcoming, is a really relaxing place to enjoy a drink, and is very popular as a result, while the accommodation is also temptingly attractive. Wetheral remains an interesting place to explore despite its recent growth, with the solid sixteenth-century church of Holy Trinity; Wetheral Priory, just to the south, a Benedictine priory with gatehouse and medieval walling remaining; and an attractive walk past three man-made caves (inhabited as late as the fourteenth century) in the rocky river bank to Cote House, where a two-storey bastle-house, with accommodation for cattle below and the farmer and his family above, is incorporated into the present farmhouse. Then, perhaps, back along the river for a well-earned pint!

MAPS

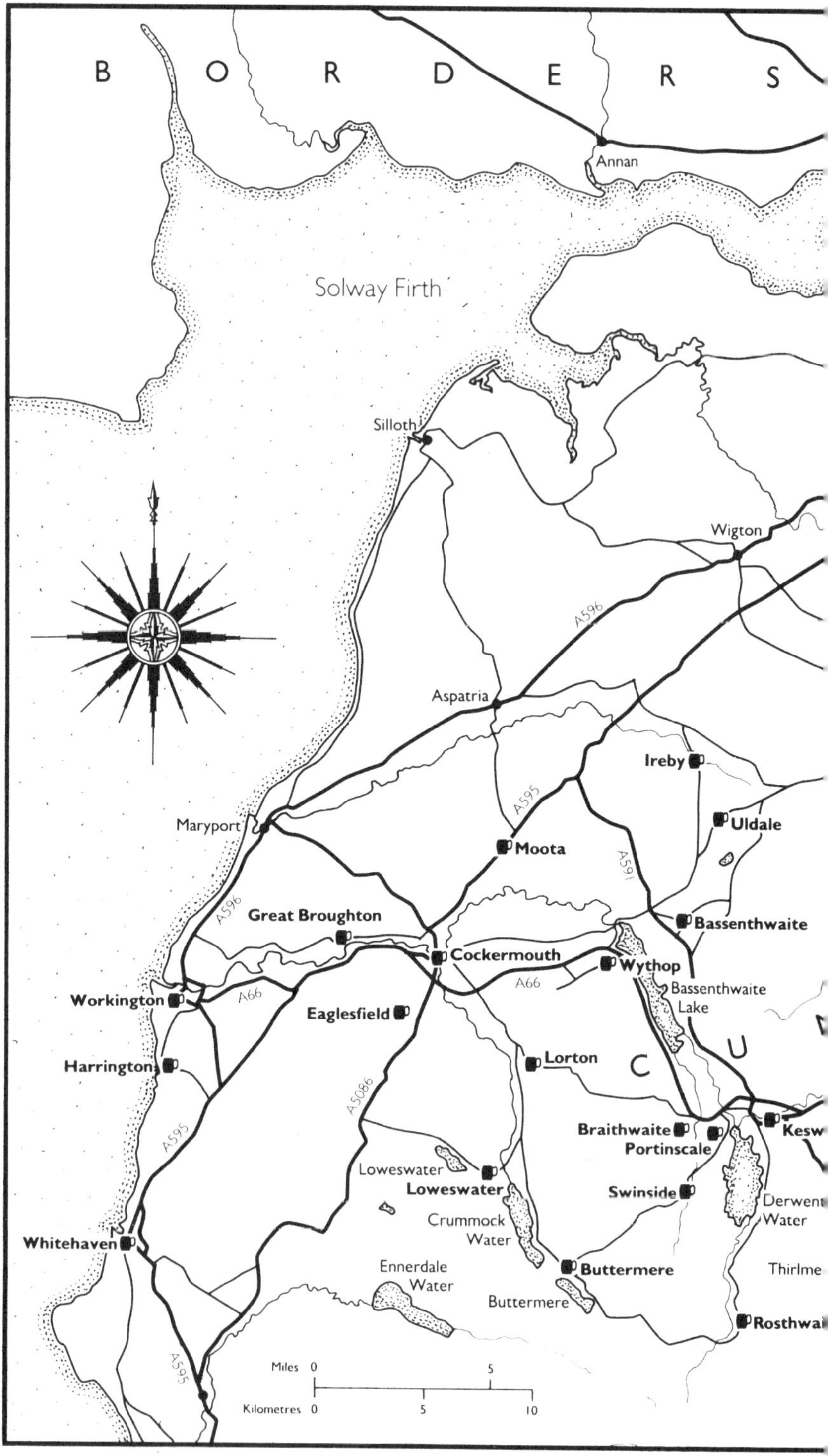
B O R D E R S
Annan
Solway Firth
Silloth
Wigton
A596
Aspatria
Ireby
Uldale
Maryport
A595
Moota
A591
A596
Great Broughton
Bassenthwaite
Cockermouth
Wythop
A66
Bassenthwaite Lake
Workington
A66
Eaglesfield
Harrington
Lorton
C U
A5086
Braithwaite
Portinscale
Kesw
A595
Loweswater
Loweswater
Swinside
Derwent Water
Crummock Water
Whitehaven
Ennerdale Water
Buttermere
Buttermere
Thirlme
Rosthwai
A595
Miles 0 5
Kilometres 0 5 10

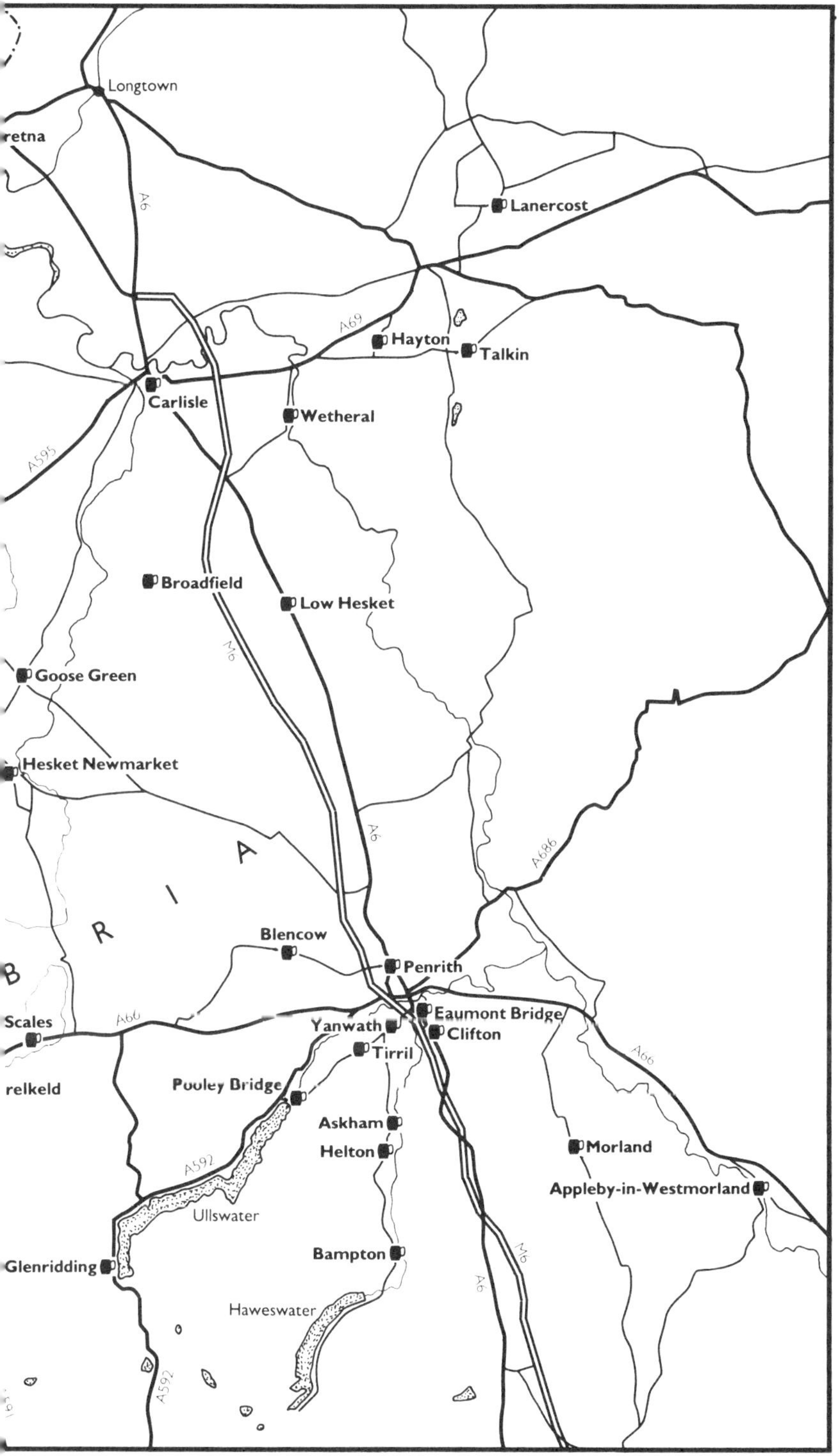

Longtown
retna
A6
Lanercost
A69
Hayton
Talkin
Carlisle
Wetheral
A595
Broadfield
Low Hesket
M6
Goose Green
Hesket Newmarket
A6
A686
B
R
I
A
Blencow
Penrith
Eaumont Bridge
Scales
A66
Yanwath
Clifton
Tirril
A66
relkeld
Pooley Bridge
Askham
Helton
Morland
Appleby-in-Westmorland
A592
Ullswater
Glenridding
Bampton
M6
A6
Haweswater
A592
Perrott Cartographics

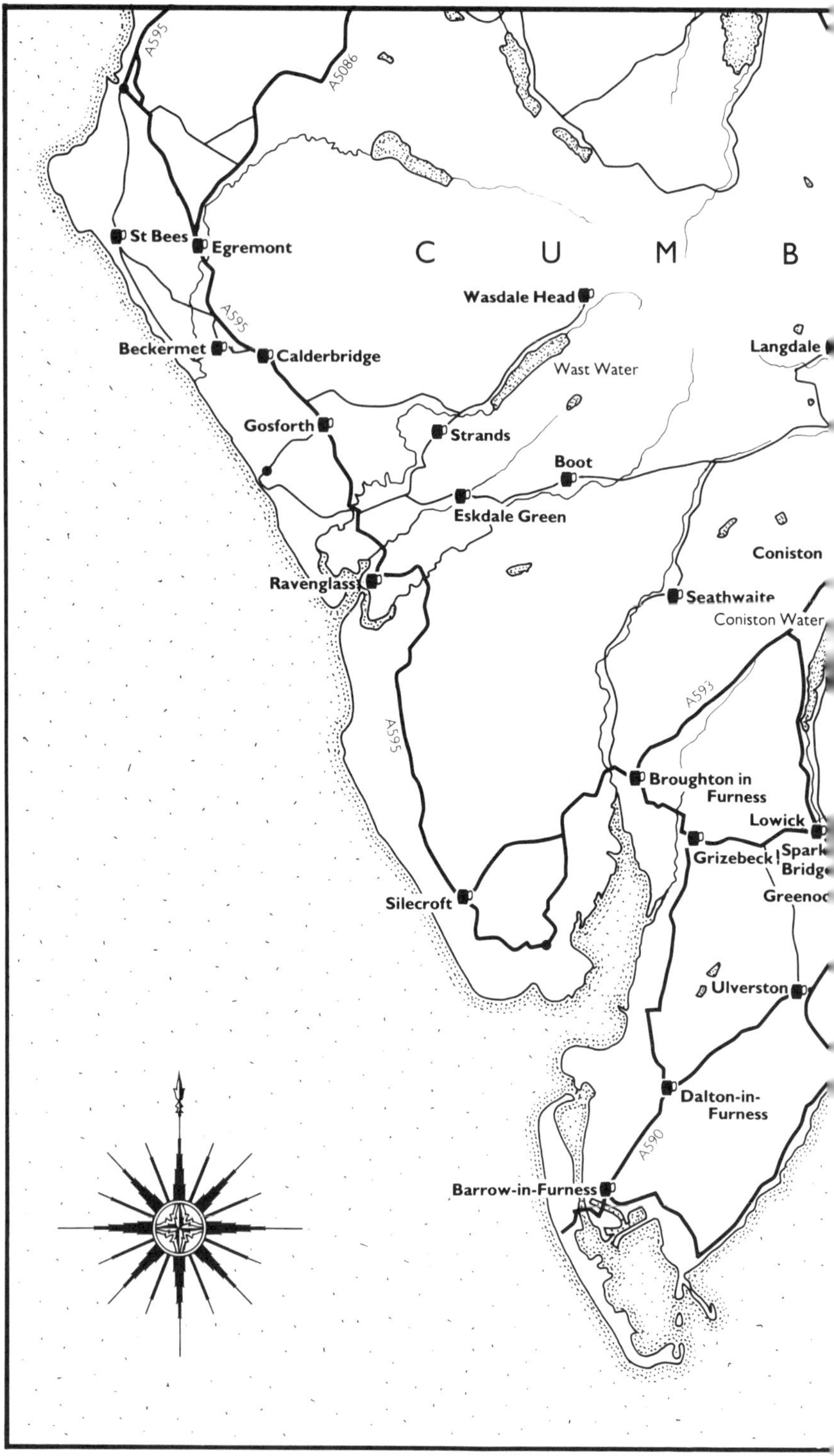
A595
A5086
St Bees
Egremont
C U M B
Wasdale Head
A595
Beckermet
Calderbridge
Langdale
Wast Water
Gosforth
Strands
Boot
Eskdale Green
Coniston
Ravenglass
Seathwaite
Coniston Water
A593
A595
Broughton in Furness
Lowick
Grizebeck
Spark Bridge
Greenod
Silecroft
Ulverston
Dalton-in-Furness
A590
Barrow-in-Furness

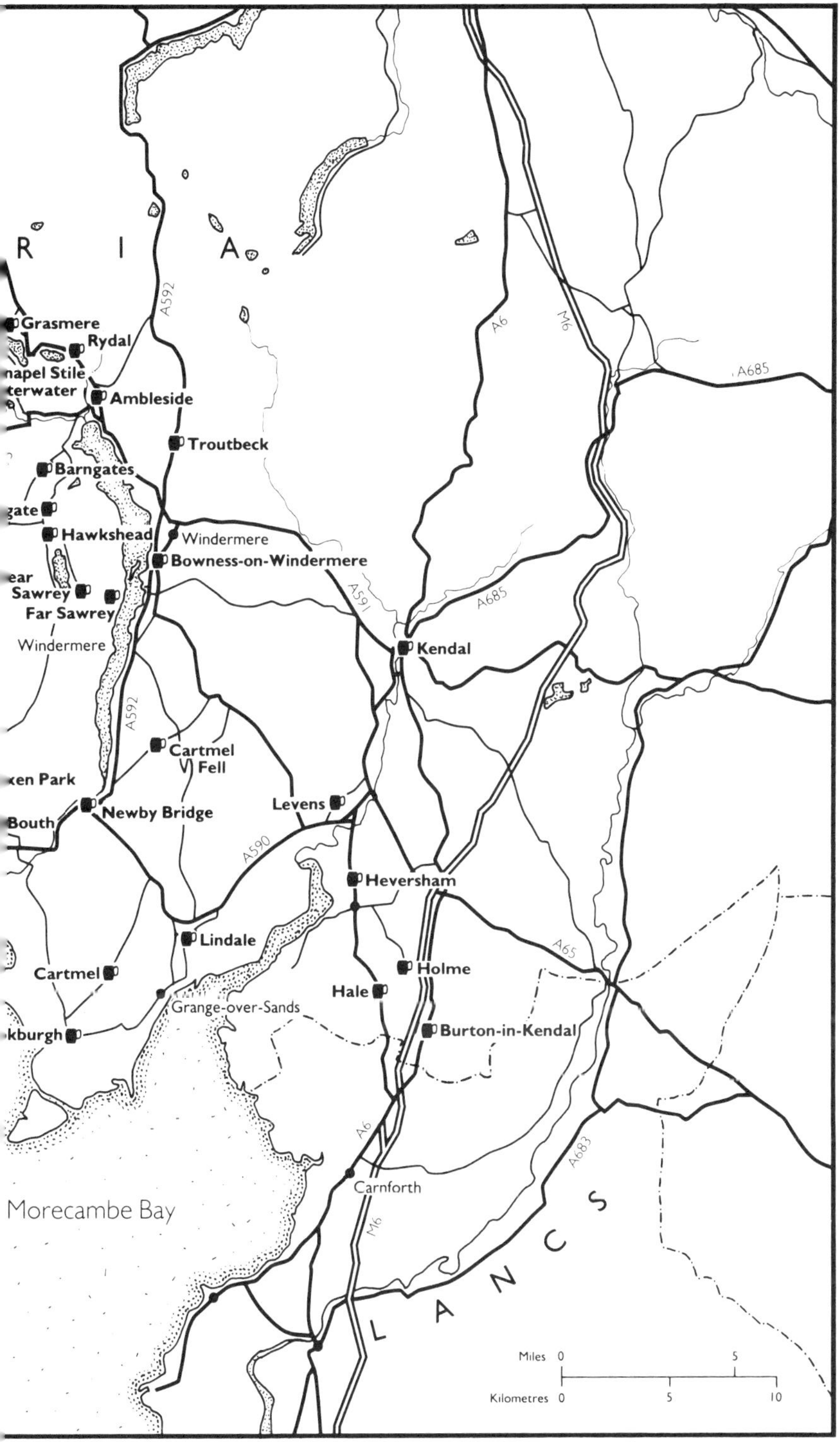

Perrott Cartographics

ALMA BOOKS

Alma Books Ltd is the publishing company set up by CAMRA (the Campaign for Real Ale) to produce titles of interest to pub-lovers, beer-drinkers, tourists and travellers. A series of regional pub guides is being developed, along with other titles covering the United Kingdom as a whole.

For more information about Alma Books and to obtain the books listed below (which are also available at all good bookshops), write to Alma Books Ltd., 34 Alma Road, St Albans, Herts. AL1 3BW.

Available now:

The Best Pubs in London **£4.95**

The Best Pubs in Devon and Cornwall **£4.95**

Companion volumes to the Lakeland guide offering the reader detailed descriptions of the finest pubs in the area.

The Good Pub Food Guide **£5.95**

Over four hundred pubs around the country where good food is as much a priority as good beer and you may find some of the best examples of traditional British cooking, using the finest local produce.

Pubs For Families **£4.95**

A nationwide listing of pubs which serve real ale, where children are not just tolerated, but really made welcome by providing good facilities including meals and play areas (indoors as well as outside).

Forthcoming attractions:

A Bedside Book of Beer

A Complete Guide to the Great British Pub

CORRECTIONS AND AMENDMENTS

Every year sees around a quarter of Lakeland pubs change hands. A new licensee can bring improvements or disaster to even the finest establishment. While most details were checked shortly before going to press, errors will inevitably occur and changes come thick and fast.

If you come upon listed pubs which have been ruined or if you find an undiscovered gem on your travels, let me know and I will investigate for the next edition.

Complete the form below or write to: Mike Dunn (Lakeland), Alma Books, 34 Alma Road, St. Albans, Hertfordshire, AL1 3BW.

County ______________________________

Town or village ______________________________

Name of pub ______________________________

Address ______________________________

Location (A or B road) ______________________________

Tel no. ____________ Name of licensee ______________________________

Description of pub (including bars, food, family room and any special facilities)

____

____

Beers ______________________________

____

____

Reasons for recommendation for inclusion in/deletion from the guide

____

____

____

Your name and address ______________________________

____

____

Postcode ______________________________

County

Town or village

Name of pub

Address

Location (A or B road)

Tel no. Name of licensee

Description of pub (including bars, food, family room and any special facilities)

Beers

Reasons for recommendation for inclusion in/deletion from the guide

Your name and address

Postcode

Join CAMRA

If you like good beer and good pubs you could be helping in the fight to preserve, protect and promote them. CAMRA was set up in the early seventies to fight against the mass destruction of a part of Britain's heritage.

The giant brewers are still pushing through takeovers, mergers and closures of their smaller regional rivals. They are still reducing the availability and diluting the quality of a magnificent and uniquely British product – real ale. They are still trying to impose national brands of beer and lager on their customers whether they like it or not, and they are still closing down town and village local pubs or converting them into grotesque 'theme' pubs.

CAMRA wants to see genuine free competition in the brewing industry, fair prices, civilised licensing laws, and, above all, a top quality product brewed by local breweries in accordance with local tastes, and served in pubs that maintain the best features of a tradition that goes back centuries.

If you are in sympathy with these aims you could be expressing that sympathy in a positive way, by joining CAMRA. We have well over 20,000 members and that's not including our three fully paid-up dogs and two cats! Yet we're pitting ourselves against the power and financial muscle of a multi-million pound, multi-national industry. We desperately need active campaigning members, but we are also grateful for the support of people whose only involvement may be to pay their membership subscription once a year. It's only £9, but each additional subscription helps us to campaign that bit more effectively across the whole spectrum of pub issues on behalf of *all* pub-users.

If you leave it to others, you may wake up one day to find *your* local pub shut, *your* local brewery closed down, *your* favourite beer no longer being brewed. So join CAMRA and help us to prove that the most important person in the brewing industry isn't the megalomaniac chairman of some brewing giant, but that most vital, and under-valued person – the pub customer.

Full membership £9 Joint husband/wife membership £9 Life membership £90 I/We wish to become members of CAMRA Ltd. I/We agree to abide by the memorandum and articles of association of the company. I/We enclose a cheque/p.o. for £9/£90.

Name(s) ______________________________

____

Address ______________________________

____

____

____

Signature(s) ______________________________

INDEX TO PUB NAMES